The Developing Child

Recent decades have witnessed unprecedented advances in research on human development. Each book in The Developing Child series reflects the importance of this research as a resource for enhancing children's well-being. It is the purpose of the series to make this resource available to that increasingly large number of people who are responsible for raising a new generation. We hope that these books will provide rich and useful information for parents, educators, child-care professionals, students of developmental psychology, and all others concerned with childhood.

Jerome Bruner, University of Oxford
Michael Cole, Rockefeller University
Barbara Lloyd, University of Sussex
Series Editors

Mothering

Rudolph Schaffer

Harvard University Press
Cambridge, Massachusetts

Library of Congress Cataloging in Publication Data
Schaffer, Rudolph, 1926-
  Mothering.
  (The Developing child)
  Bibliography: p.
  Includes index.
  1. Mother and child. 2. Infant psychology.
I. Title. II. Series.
BF723.P25S32   155.4'18   76-56852
ISBN 0-674-58745-6 (cloth)
ISBN 0-674-58746-4 (paper)

Contents

Credits

The
Developing
Child

Mothering

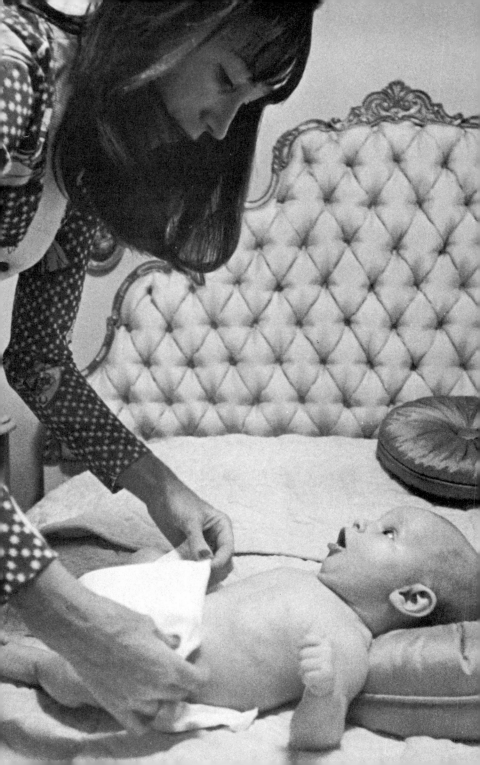

1 / Introduction

What is mothering? What are mothers for, what are their functions, and what influences do they have on children? For that matter, who are mothers—is this a role based on sex and parturition, or can it be extended beyond these limits? At first sight, answers to such questions may seem obvious, for we are dealing with one of the universals of mankind—a relationship that occurs naturally, runs its course spontaneously, and of which everyone has some personal knowledge. And so we tend to take it for granted, explain it as being based on instinct, and shrug off instances of maternal neglect and cruelty as the kind of occasional aberration that may occur in any universal pattern.

And yet, on closer examination, there is nothing simple or straightforward about mothering. List the different activities a mother performs in the course of any one day with her child, and their range—from nose wiping to rocking, from offering the breast to scolding—will be truly astounding. Then take any one of these actions and consider its variation from one mother to the next—in its style of expression, its emotional intensity, its frequency of occurrence, and any other such characteristic as may be influenced by culture, class, setting, and individual personality. Underlying this great diversity there is, of course, considerable communality, some of which we may well share with other species. The smoothness of the relationship between a mother and her baby would, after all, hardly be possible were it not for biologically based regularities. But whereas in some lower species a mother's activities may be almost wholly determined by innate mechanisms—and therefore largely stereotyped in expression—humans are outstanding in their ability to adapt their

1

behavior in the light of acquired self-knowledge. To add to that self-knowledge is the goal of psychology and the justification for the scientific study of mothering.

Mothering, then, is a highly complex pattern, the more so because it involves *two* individuals. To do justice to the interactive quality, as well as to the range of activities and the diversity of their expression, is clearly no simple task. No wonder so many different conceptions of the essence of mothering have been put forward: mother has variously been seen as teacher, lover, guide, judge, dictator, seducer, model, lion tamer, provider of food, and protector against danger. To say she is all of these is both true and useless—true, because she indeed fulfills these (and other) functions; useless, because such a catalogue can give but little indication of the nature of the interaction by means of which the child first becomes assimilated into the social world.

What goes on between child and parent is of concern to many. For the practitioner in social work, education, or medicine, the challenge lies in searching for ways to improve the conditions under which children are reared during the early years of life and thus—one hopes—being in a better position to prevent children from becoming ill or deviant or not using their natural talents. For the social scientist there is the opportunity of learning about the origins of behavior and picking up some of the clues that may explain how personality is formed. And for the parent there is the very personal motive of wanting to find out about himself and learning the "right" way of bringing up children.

In recent times a whole industry has sprung up to cater to the parental market. Soothsayers galore publish weekly columns in women's magazines on bringing up children, or reach fame and fortune with one of the many "baby books" now so widely available. Clearly these avuncular experts do fulfill some important function, if only to bring solace to confused and puzzled parents in search of certainty. Yet what they say is rarely based on anything other than some branch of currently prevalent common-sense, supplemented perhaps by personal experience of the untypical few who wind their way through their consulting rooms; it is certainly not based on systematically obtained knowledge derived from objective research. Go through Dr. Spock's *Baby and Child Care* and see how much of that is based on established fact rather than personal prejudice—however kindly intentioned!

Examine a weekly advice column and note the unproven assumptions and the value judgments underlying its statements! No wonder such advice is subject to swings of fashion every bit as unpredictable as those in *haute couture;* no wonder "experts" suddenly change their minds, much to the consternation of generations brought up along the lines formerly advocated. Within the space of just a decade or two parents were first sternly warned by the Truby King movement against the dangers of spoiling, undue affection, and insufficient firmness, only then to be subjected to a barrage of psychoanalytically derived pronouncements about the horrific consequences of thwarting and disciplining one's child. Should infant feeding be scheduled or self-demand, thumbsucking permitted or not? Should a baby be picked up when crying or be left? Surely it is better to have objective information on these practices—based on planned investigation into the immediate and subsequent effects.

Unfortunately the notion that the scientist has a place in the nursery, that his findings may not only be used to understand the parent-child relationship but also be applied to its conduct, has been slow to gain recognition and is still considered by some as preposterous. Is not the relationship sacrosanct, a private matter that can only be degraded by the intrusion of the psychologist? Is it not impossible for the scientist ever to capture the flavor of something as subtle and emotionally laden as mother love?

These objections need to be taken seriously. In part no doubt they derive from a fear of psychological inquiry generally, which by its very nature seems an invasion of privacy. Such feelings are reminiscent of the objections (mainly religious) in medieval times to the dissection of the human body, and no doubt psychologists will overcome such apprehensions in due course just as anatomists have. If what at first sight appears to be an assault on human dignity turns out to be motivated by a wish to help and improve, endeavors such as "baby watching" will become generally acceptable—particularly as psychologists are now no longer just writing for fellow scientists, merely to add to existing knowledge. There is now a growing acknowledgment that the ultimate consumers are the parents themselves, together with their children, and that the ultimate aim is action as well as knowledge. And if that action is to bring about change with regard to issues of current social concern—issues such as separation, or day care, or the role of the father—then the consumer must be involved in the research effort from the beginning, for change cannot be imposed by decree. Parents are then no longer just "subjects" but partners in a joint enterprise to which they themselves see some point.

As to the fear that scientific inquiry will rob what it studies of mystique, this cannot be denied—on the contrary, that is its very aim. Mystique is the province of the poet, the painter, the novelist; artistic treatment of, say, mother love may well lead to a deeper appreciation of its emotional intensity, but only detached analysis can bring about the type of understanding on which therapeutic action is based. And for the parent, information derived from scientific sources need no more convert the care of his child from an art to a science than knowledge of the color spectrum need take away the creative element from the artist's task. Art can be informed and still remain a spontaneous expression of the individual's personality.

Nor need it be feared that the end result of scientific inquiry is to reduce the diversity of parental practices to one formula—to produce recipes for childrearing that are mandatory for all. Few are now so ethnocentric as to believe that middle-class Western parental behavior is the norm to which all others should conform, that the Mundugumor of New Guinea or the bushmen of the Kalahari Desert are "wrong" in the way they bring up their children and need to be converted. Tolerance of such diversity and care to avoid rash value judgments are clearly essential. "Deficit models," whereby, for instance, the speech of lower-class American blacks is regarded as *inferior* English rather than as a distinctive dialect, are increasingly being called into question. Yet the danger is that we go too far in the opposite direction and, in accepting everything, no longer feel impelled to take action to ameliorate conditions that clearly do not permit a child to reach his full potential. If, for example, it is true that children brought up in linguistically impoverished environments later perform poorly at communication and problem solving, it is surely right to take remedial action. If, on the other hand, research can uncover no clear-cut differences between the children of working and nonworking mothers, it would be improper to give advice to mothers that goes against their own personal inclination. In the former case there is a "right" way; not in the latter. Only research can tell us what the "absolutes" in childrearing are.

When a child enters school at the age of five or six, it is widely agreed that the educational techniques he meets are a matter of public concern, that they need to be systematically scrutinized in relation to the effects they produce, and that the results of such inquiry should inform the teacher's classroom behavior. There is, in fact, no reason why bringing up the under-fives should not also be guided by firm knowledge scientifically established rather than depend, as happens at present, on fashion, prejudice, and what grandmother says. The parent-child relationship need be no more immune from properly conducted objective inquiry than the movements of the planets or the structure of DNA— even if its analysis presents problems of far greater complexity.

In view of this complexity it is not surprising to find that in the last few decades investigators have employed various approaches to untangle the mothering process. These approaches may be thought of as different research strategies, each concentrating on a distinct aspect of the mothering process—which they consider to represent its essence—and each coming up with its own conclusions as to what is important and what is not. The four principal approaches with which I shall be concerned may be characterized as "mothering as physical care," "mothering as a set of attitudes," "mothering as stimulation," and "mothering as interlocution." My interest will center especially on the last two, for most of the more recent findings are subsumed there. Yet the other two, to which I shall turn first, have also provided some valuable lessons.

My concern will primarily be with the description and analysis of mothering in the child's earliest years, regardless of who actually carries on this process. I shall not follow the current vogue for the label "parenting," for though the implied inclusion of father is welcome, the gain in restricting the term to two specified individuals rather than to one is hardly sufficient to make up for its contrived nature. I shall later take up the question of who "mother" is; until then mother may be thought of as anyone with responsibility for the child's care over a prolonged period.

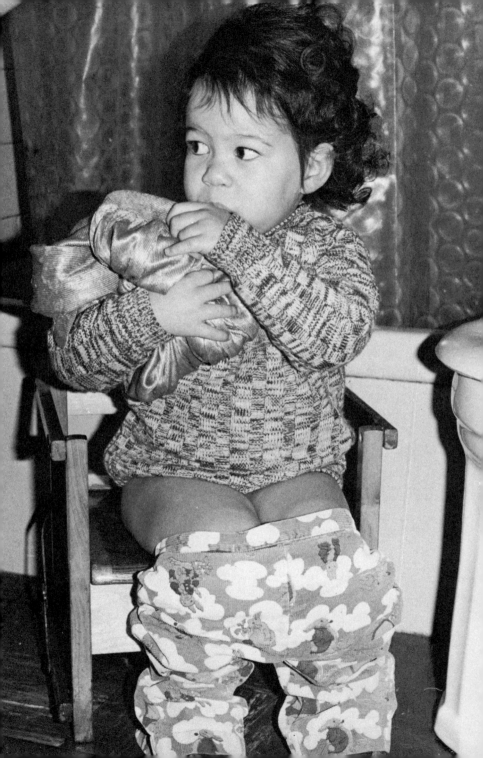

2 / Childrearing and Early Experience

What happens in childhood is of interest for two reasons: first, because we wish to find out about children as such; second, because we believe that events early in life play an important part in shaping adult personality.

The first needs no justification. Whether our interest is practical or theoretical, whether we set out to provide the "correct" treatment for children of various ages or whether we wish to understand the processes underlying their behavior, we must describe and experiment systematically and objectively in order to arrive at worthwhile conclusions. What kind of toys ought one to design for one-year-olds? Is it realistic to teach three-year-olds number concepts? How and when does the child learn to control his aggressive impulses? There are many such questions which all those in contact with children can pose and which the psychologist can in due course be expected to answer. The search for better methods of child care and of education, and indeed for ways of simply "keeping happy," needs no excuse.

The second reason for an interest in child development is perhaps not so self-evident. It is contained in the aphorism "the child is father of the man," and expresses the belief that a child's experiences in the early years will leave a mark on him for the rest of his life. The explanation for adult personality, in other words, is to be found in the individual's first encounters with the world, at a time when he is thought to be in a highly impressionable state. And these encounters, of course, involve primarily the mother.

THE SEARCH FOR THE DETERMINANTS
OF PERSONALITY

The belief that early experience determines adult behavior is so widespread that it may well be regarded as commonsense. Probably most parents subscribe to this view, and while they may not deliberately choose particular methods of child care to bring about a specified long-term outcome, their belief in the association may well make them feel an added responsibility.

But what of the actual evidence to justify this belief? Much of it has come from work with animals, for here it is possible to arrange particular experiences at particular ages and subsequently test for their effect on the behavior of mature animals. Thus infant mice have been subjected to electric-shock treatment and their emotionality assessed later on in comparison with nonshocked animals. Chimpanzees have been reared in darkness for varying periods after birth in order to test their subsequent perceptual capacity. Dogs kept in isolation as puppies have been compared with normally reared animals on various problem-solving tasks. And in one experiment rats were exposed throughout infancy to the music of either Mozart or Schoenberg and then given musical preference tests in adulthood (with the result that animals brought up on Mozart showed a definite preference for that music, whereas the Schoenberg-reared group gave no indication of a hankering after the familiar music!). Much of this work does show a definite effect: though there are still many questions about the precise links between early events and subsequent outcomes in various species, belief in the compelling nature of early experience is powerfully reinforced by this body of findings.

Yet what applies to a rat or dog need not hold for a human being. Unfortunately the evidence here is so far much more sparse and much less clear, for experiments with children raise obvious ethical problems—at least when they involve such extreme treatments as isolation, shock, or Schoenberg. "Experiments of nature," the naturally occurring fluctuations of life experience, have therefore been resorted to, but though these have raised some intriguing questions they have so far provided few conclusive answers. Does the first relationship established by the child serve as a prototype for all subsequent relationships? Do nuances within this relationship continue to reverberate throughout life? Are the daily frustrations encountered by the infant traumata that irreversibly shape his behavior? These are ambitious questions, whose answers might have considerable implications for the way parents approach childrearing.

MOTHERING AS PHYSICAL CARE

Freud, more than any other writer, believed in the importance of early experience. However, he was not content merely to make the general assertion; he went further in stipulating the kinds of experience that will produce particular kinds of results if encountered at specified stages of development. Thus, according to Freud's "libidinal theory," the child progresses through a number of phases (oral, anal, genital), in the course of which he is particularly sensitive to certain kinds of stimulation. During the oral phase, extending over the first year or so of life, his main concerns involve activities like sucking, swallowing, and biting; and the nature of his oral experiences during this period will have considerable repercussions in the long as well as the short term. Should they generally be gratifying, he will successfully pass through that phase to the next one; should they be frustrating he will remain fixated at this stage and as an adult manifest a particular personality constellation, the "oral character," distinguished by such features as excessive dependence, passivity, and "mouth habits." Similarly, the child fixated at the anal stage will develop an "anal character," whose most marked traits are said to be orderliness, parsimony, and obstinacy.

Adult personality is thus directly related to the way in which infantile physiological urges are channeled. Whether the child receives the breast or a bottle, whether he is fed according to demand or by schedule, the age at which he is weaned and how suddenly, and the severity of his toilet training—these are the kinds of influences that Freud considered to be major determinants of personality growth. Variations in such practices would therefore account for later behavior.

Such a theory, predicting associations between childhood and adult features, is important on at least two grounds. First, it would help us to understand why people differ from one another and firmly point out the causes of these differences. And second, if borne out, it would enable parents to choose ι .ιong particular infant-care practices and foster the kind of personality they wish.

Investigating Freud's Theories. Unfortunately Freud's evidence for his propositions were somewhat indirect, being derived from the "memories" of adult patients, whose difficulties and characteristics he believed could best be accounted for by the libidinal theory. At best, therefore, Freud's views must be regarded as suggestions that need to be followed up by systematic research.

Accordingly, during the 1930s and 1940s a large number of psychologists turned their attention to just this. Does breastfeeding leave the child with some sort of psychological advantage over bottle-fed children? Is self-demand feeding more likely to produce a confident and nonneurotic personality than rigidly scheduled feeding? Is early weaning a traumatic event whose effects will last for life? Are there indeed links between toilet training and the anal character? These and other such questions occupied developmental research workers for a long while, and their results were eventually pulled together in a number of reviews, such as that by Bettye Caldwell.[1]

Their conclusions may be summarized quite simply: there is no evidence to show that specific infant-care practices have an unvarying psychological effect on the child that manifests itself in later years. Freud's hypotheses are not upheld: if the child is father of the man it is for reasons other than missing out on the breast and a too early acquaintance with the potty.

Why this failure? It is true that many of the experiments in this area were grossly inadequate in method: they failed to ensure that the individuals they studied were similar, apart from the single factor being scrutinized; they relied unduly on mothers' memories for information about early events; their various findings could not be compared because of disagreement about what should be counted as "early weaning" or "harsh training," and so on. Yet this alone cannot account for the negative results, for the weight of evidence is such that the general conclusion can hardly be challenged.

Any investigation that covers a long span of time is bound to encounter certain special problems. In particular, if one is examining the effects of some early experience on adult behavior, one must take into account the events in the intervening period. One might wish to examine the effects of the father's death during a child's early years on the development of masculinity, and accordingly compare a group of adolescent boys who had this experience with a group who did not. To do so without taking into account whether, within the former group, the mother remarried or not, or whether or not uncles, grandfathers, or older brothers were able to step into the gap and provide the child with male company, would be to neglect some possible important influences. Investigations with animals avoid this problem, for there one can ensure that the "treated" and the "untreated" groups would have identical intervening experience. Human beings, on the other hand, can hardly be so regimented.

It may be argued that the effects of physical-care experiences, though obscured later on by subsequent events, do at least have an impact *at the time*, and that much of the variation in *infant* behavior can be accounted for by differences in training practices. In fact, even this association has not been clearly upheld. To take one example: it has frequently been said that a child's attachment to his mother develops out of his physical dependence on her. In the early months of life, according to this view, he learns that she provides food and other bodily comforts, therefore comes to value her presence, and in due course will want her in her own right. If this is so, it should follow that the more gratifying a mother's physical-care practices are, the greater should be the child's developing attachment to her. Peggy Emerson and I tested this association.[2] We took measures of the intensity of attachment of eighteen-month-old infants to their mothers and related them to measures of feeding rigidity, age at weaning, length of the weaning period, age when toilet training began, and severity of toilet training. We found no relationship in any case. We noted, moreover, how infants sometimes form strong attachments to fathers, grandparents, and older siblings who may never have participated in routine care. Clearly the view that sociability arises primarily in the context of feeding cannot be upheld; the physical-care experiences examined cannot account for variations in behavior—not even behavior at the time.

To the psychologist searching for the determinants of personality this sort of outcome is disappointing; to the parent, on the other hand, it should be good news. If personality were irreversibly fixed by particular childrearing practices the individual would remain forever at the mercy of specific experiences in his past. As it is, mothers can be assured that their decision to bottle-feed rather than breast-feed their baby (to take one example) is highly unlikely per se to have any implications for his personality in later years. Even during infancy itself, whatever the *physical* advantages of breastfeeding, there are no distinctive psychological concomitants. The same applies to the other aspects of early physical care: nature, it appears, has arranged things rather more flexibly and kindly than Freud believed.

MOTHERING AS A SET OF ATTITUDES

The practices discussed so far refer mainly to specific events experienced by the child at specific ages. It may be, however, that the reason for the failure to link these up with child behavior is that they are *too* specific, and that they are given meaning only in the wider context of parental attitudes. The fact that a baby is weaned early, according to this argument, matters less than the reason for this decision: whether it reflects a cultural norm, or stems from the mother's revulsion at physical intimacy, or expresses an urge to hurry the child toward independence. Is the child accepted or rejected, brought up in a tolerant or intolerant atmosphere? Does he encounter warm or cold relationships in the home? These are more pervasive influences, not usually confined to any one time, and may be said to define the personal milieu in which the child spends his early years. One and the same practice may be performed by a nurturant or a hostile mother, may occur within an easygoing or a rigidly authoritarian home, or may take place against a background of love or of hate. Perhaps these are the crucial influences that shape the child's personality development.

Parental attitudes and their measurement. During the 1950s and early 1960s a lot of effort was devoted to attempts, in the first place, to identify and measure parental attitudes and, in the second place, to relate them to characteristics of child behavior. Thus a great deal of psychometric expertise went into constructing questionnaires and interview schedules that would yield clear-cut dimensions along which parents could be ranged. For example, in what was a most influential study at the time, Robert Sears, Eleanor Maccoby, and Harry Levin obtained reports from the mothers of 379 five-year-olds on the rearing practices they had adopted at various phases of their children's lives.[3] They asked not only about feeding, weaning, and toileting practices, but also about such matters as the mothers' ways of handling dependent and aggressive behavior, their methods of disciplining, their feelings toward pregnancy, overt expression of affection, and adjustment in marriage. They also asked about the children's behavior.

A number of dimensions of childrearing emerged from this material, and of these two are worth special mention because they have been found by other investigators too. The first dimension has been labeled *warmth-coldness* and is based on, for instance, the affection the mother shows the child, the extent to which she is demonstratively playful, her acceptance of the child's dependency, and her use of reasoning in disciplining him. The second dimension, *permissiveness-restrictiveness*, describes, for instance, her tolerance of aggressive and sexual behavior, her insistence on good manners and obedience, and her use of physical punishment.

Perhaps the most notable of other attempts to describe parents in this fashion was undertaken by Earl S. Schaefer.[4] It was based on the construction of a questionnaire, the Parental Attitude Research Inventory (PARI), in which parents were asked to indicate their agreement with such statements as "A child will be grateful later on for strict training," and "Children should realize how much parents have to give up for them." Again two main dimensions emerged from parents' answers, called *love-hostility* and *control-autonomy* but referring essentially to the same features as the dimensions described by Sears and his colleagues.

Thus a "model" of parental characteristics was put forward, in which the combination of the two independent dimensions yielded four types of parents. It is true that other investigators found further dimensions which they considered important (such as *emotional involvement-calm detachment*), yet by and large the above two were confirmed by most.

However, the difficulties of this approach became apparent in attempts to relate these parental characteristics to child behavior. Sears, Maccoby, and Levin had described a great many such relationships: the greatest upset in children resulting from severe toilet training, for example, was found when it was combined with a cold, undemonstrative attitude on the part of the mother; children experiencing some rejection tended to show more dependent behavior than accepted children; the greatest aggressiveness resulted from a combination of a highly permissive attitude and occasional severe punishment, and so on. These findings were widely accepted as "true" and universally representative. To warrant such claims, however, results must, at the very least, be replicable, and in this respect they failed. When Marian Radke Yarrow, John Campbell, and Roger Burton used the same techniques to examine dependence, aggression, and conscience formation, they were unable to confirm the findings previously obtained.[5] At the same time, it became increasingly apparent that research using instruments like the PARI was not producing clear-cut relationships: on the basis of attitudinal measures alone it has proved difficult to predict child personality. Parental attitudes, like early physical-care practices, have not turned out to be the clear-cut determinants of personality development one had hoped for.

What went wrong with attitude research?　There are a number of reasons to account for this conclusion. In the first place, there is a gap between *say* and *do:* however cooperative a mother, it may be genuinely difficult for her to provide undistorted information about her behavior and feelings as they impinge on her child. There are ways of minimizing such distortions but, in questionnaires about childrearing especially, "social desirability" tends to play a large part in determining the answers given. No wonder that comparisons between questionnaires on attitudes and direct observations of behavior have produced few significant results: in one study, for example, there were fewer correlations between the two than one would expect by chance! And as far as the child is concerned, it is the mother's *behavior* that will impinge on him, not some abstract concept.

In the second place, the correlations that are produced are merely statements about associations and tell us nothing about the direction of cause and effect. Yet parental attitudes have generally been treated as though they cause children's behavior. As we shall see, children are just as capable of affecting parents, thus producing a much more complex picture of the interaction.

Finally, an attitudinal measure represents a highly summarized statement. To say that a mother is permissive neglects the fact that her attitude may vary from one area of behavior to another: she may be highly permissive about behavior toward visitors and yet utterly intolerant when it comes to toileting. An attitude may, moreover, fluctuate over time, being influenced by experience as to what works. And, in addition, attitudinal studies have tended to neglect the setting in which mother and child interact: the fact that physical punishment occurs at mealtimes does not necessarily tell us anything about its use at bedtime.

Summary statements are useful in everyday speech, where we are continually describing people as intelligent or aggressive or generous or nice. In the reports of social workers, psychiatrists, or teachers, such global terms can hardly be avoided; for them the labels and importance attached by research workers to facets of parental behavior are likely to be of considerable use. We see how limited these global concepts are, though, when we expect them to tell us something about how children will actually behave. This they cannot do, mainly because they take out of context the parental characteristics they are studying and then average out all fluctuations over time and situation. Attitudes were originally selected as possible determinants of child development because they were of a general and abstract nature; but their use as anything but abbreviated labels has now been abandoned just because they are so abstract and general.

IS EARLY EXPERIENCE IMPORTANT?

What are we to conclude about the implications for his later personality of the way in which a child is treated during his early years? Are early experiences of special significance just because they are early, and is the child more malleable at that time?

The notion that parents can exert a particularly profound influence during the first few years—an influence that will remain throughout life and cannot be eradicated by subsequent experience—is certainly widespread. At its most extreme form it was expressed by J. B. Watson in 1925: "Give me a dozen healthy infants, well formed, and my own specified world to bring them up in, and I will guarantee to take any one at random and train him to become any type of specialist I might select—doctor, lawyer, artist, merchant chief, and yes, even beggarman and thief, regardless of his talents, penchants, tendencies, abilities, vocations, and the race of his ancestors."[6] There may be few today who are quite so confident about the precision with which children can be shaped; yet with respect to at least one of the above vocations, that of thief, many current theories of delinquency still concur that the roots of the condition are to be sought in the child's early years. And, more generally, faith in the permanently formative influences of the child's first encounters with the world persists among both parents and professional workers.

Yet faith rather than fact is what such a belief is built on. Human development is rather more complicated, rather less rigidly determined than such a view suggests. Although one would dearly like more supportive evidence, what we have so far indicates that isolated experiences rarely if ever leave permanent traces—however traumatic and however early they may be. And perhaps this is just as well, for were it not so, and were we to believe that personality became irreversibly set in the first two, three, or five years of life we should have to believe, first, that any child harmed then was beyond help and thus clinically not worth bothering about; and, second, that children in later years were not vulnerable and that experience then was of no consequence. Both beliefs would be highly dangerous if translated into practice: they overvalue the effects of early experience and undervalue the role of later experience. This danger is well demonstrated by the early efforts made to help culturally disadvantaged children, many of which simply provided each child with a dose of relevant training during the preschool period in the expectation that this on its own would give him the required extras for normal cognitive development. The speedy "washout" effect that set in showed clearly how unrealistic it is to expect the developmental course to be changed when just one period is singled out for attention and no effort is made to follow up that experience and integrate it in an individual's total life pattern.

Continuity and discontinuity in development. It is easy to assert that a child's early experience is important, but considerably more difficult to substantiate. What experience? How early? Important in what way?

The belief in the overriding role of early experience has usually been based, implicitly or explicitly, on a "critical-period model," which suggests that there are fixed developmental stages during which the child or animal is particularly sensitive to certain influences. The clearest example of such sensitivity is the "imprinting" phenomenon. According to early ethological studies, it seemed that the young of certain birds like ducks and chickens would follow the first moving object they met and form a lasting attachment to it; also that this attachment could take place only within a sharply limited period early on in development and that it would affect all subsequent relationships. If, for instance, the animal became imprinted on a tennis ball it might subsequently attempt to mate with other tennis balls. If it were kept isolated during the critical period, nothing would prevent it from becoming an affectionless psychopath for the remainder of its life.

Let us first note, however, that ethologists no longer find such an all-or-none view tenable—even when applied to lower animals like ducks. The limits of critical periods have not been found to be as immutable as was formerly thought, for by manipulating the animal's experience they can be extended considerably. Nor is the learning that occurs at that time as immediate and permanent as was previously thought, for much depends on the precise experience itself. As a result, the term "sensitive period" has come to be preferred: it seems, as Robert Hinde has put it,[7] that we are merely concerned with changing *probabilities* of certain forms of learning, and that periods of maximum probability may be surrounded by periods of reduced probability.

When we turn to human development, there is even more doubt about the usefulness of the critical-period concept. It is certainly true that the individual is more sensitive to particular types of influence at some developmental stages than at others, but to say that tells us little, either about the extent to which the period can be shifted or about the reasons for the increased sensitivity.

The main problem, however, is a methodological one, for in human development specific events to which one may wish to attribute some formative influence hardly ever occur on their own but are usually embedded in a continuing context, a whole network of associated influences. Thus the death of his father is not an event that impinges on a child only at one particular point: it may go on producing shock waves through its continuing effect on the mother, which in turn may bring about a different relationship with the child; in addition there may be economic difficulties as a result of which the mother has to go out to work, a new home has to be found, and an altogether new lifestyle adopted. One event may thus produce a multitude of effects that continue to reverberate for many years. To attribute any subsequent pathology in the child to that single event would be misleading, for it is but one link in a chain of traumata, any one of which—or, more likely, the sum total of all—may be responsible for the child's condition. No wonder investigators have found it more profitable to examine this problem in animals, where it is much easier to program experience and ensure that only single events are studied without the influence of others.

We can now appreciate why care has to be taken in making statements about the role of the child's first relationship and its influence on later personality development. To suggest, for example, that adult maturity is built on a foundation of "basic trust" that must be established in infancy (as Erik Erikson did[8]) is to put forward an interesting idea which is, in practice, extraordinarily difficult to substantiate. The odds are that a relationship that engenders such trust in infancy will continue to engender it in later childhood too, and who is to say at the end of it all that one period was more crucial than another in bringing about the final result? Similarly where no such trust has been brought about—if, say, a child's family disintegrates—it may well be but the beginning of a whole sequence of misfortunes and unsatisfactory care arrangements in institutions and foster homes.

Just occasionally, however, drastic discontinuities in a child's upbringing do occur and are thus of special interest in attempts to understand the role of early experience. One such example is provided by Wayne Dennis, who observed infants reared in a crèche in Lebanon.[9] There, as the result of a regimen which involved very little adult attention, few toys, and being left all day in bed in a bare room, the infants suffered extreme deprivation. When tested at the end of the first year, they were found to have developed on average at about half the rate that is usual, though there were indications that at birth they had been potentially normal. Some of these children were subsequently adopted and, when followed up some years later, showed a remarkable recovery, with an average IQ of 85. Those adopted before the age of two years had an average IQ as high as 96, while those adopted later scored around 80. The children not adopted stayed in the original crèche until they reached the age of six, when they were transferred to two other institutions for boys and girls respectively. The girls' institution was just as restrictive in its general regimen and just as impoverished in its provision of personal attention as the creche. When tested at ages twelve to sixteen years, these girls were found to have an average IQ of 54. Thus they had remained at the same level of retardation throughout their childhood. The boys' institution, on the other hand, was run on very different lines, providing far more stimulation and facilities like play and educational equipment, film shows, and trips outside the institution. These boys, when tested, were found to have an average IQ of 80, thus showing a significant degree of recovery from the level reached at the end of the first year. Both the adopted children and the institutionalized boys show that the deprivation of intellectual and social experience in infancy had not produced irreversible consequences, however drastic the effects at the time.

Our second example comes from observations by Jerome Kagan and Robert Klein of a group of Guatemalan children living in an Indian village in an isolated, mountainous area of the country.[10] Again discontinuity of experience marks the lives of these children, despite the fact that they remain in their own homes all along. The discontinuity this time stems from the childrearing practices found in this particular setting. During infancy children tend to be kept most of the time in the small, dark interior of their hut, where they are rarely allowed to crawl on the floor, are rarely spoken to or played with (though always kept near the mother), and where few objects for play are available. If the mother travels to market she leaves the infant behind, as the outside sun, air, and dust are considered harmful. Observations of these infants revealed a picture of alarming pathology: they hardly moved, were fearful, barely smiled, and were extraordinarily quiet. Many would not turn to a sound, nor would they smile or babble when spoken to. Various tests suggested gross retardation by the end of the first year. In short, these infants were very like those in the Lebanese crèche.

Yet this depressing picture turns out to be quite unpredictive of later development. In their second year these children become able to walk, they leave the hut, and begin to participate in the life outside. All at once the range of available experiences is vastly increased, and it is not long before the apathetic, listless, and relatively incompetent infant is transformed into an active, gay, intellectually capable child. In other words these Guatemalan children show, as do Dennis' institutionalized infants, that retardation during the first year or two of life is reversible and that early experiences, however drastic at the time, do not necessarily set up patterns of behavior that cannot subsequently be modified.

Predicting developmental outcome. The above two examples give body to the suggestion by Alan Clarke that early learning, in itself, is of no more consequence than learning at any other stage of development, and that it will bring about long-term effects only if it is repeatedly reinforced throughout subsequent childhood.[11] Without that reinforcement, early learning will fade: single delimited experiences rarely produce permanent effects. In a similar vein, B. A. Campbell and J. Jaynes have argued that an early experience can be perpetuated and incorporated into the adult personality only if it is periodically *reinstated;* that is, if a small amount of partial practice, or repetition of the experience, occurs throughout childhood.[12] This applies, presumably, to the case where one misfortune sets in train a whole sequence of further misfortunes, each confirming the child's expectation of what life has to offer him and each giving him further reason to adopt whatever behavior—flight from reality, antisocial tendencies, and so forth—he used as a way of dealing with the original situation. Under such circumstances one can predict the final outcome with rather more confidence, for a child in this situation is sustained and encouraged in the response he originally adopted.

But just how constant is a child's environment, even under the most normal circumstances? It may take drastic discontinuities, of the kind described above, to highlight the fact that the environment over a period must be taken into account before one can attempt to predict the course of personality development. Yet children reared in normal home circumstances are generally regarded as remaining under such constant environmental conditions that this consideration does not hold. Mother, in other words, is thought to be always the same mother; parental influences are regarded as invariable throughout childhood, and an assessment of the parents' psychological characteristics at one point is thought sufficient to typecast them for good. Can we really take it for granted that parents are so utterly changeless in their behavior and attitudes to their children? Those few studies (we shall look at some of them in a later chapter) that have reassessed parental characteristics at various ages of the child have shown that, even in the course of a few months during infancy, there may be drastic changes in a mother's behavior—sometimes resulting from changes in the infant's behavior, sometimes brought about by extraneous factors. A mother, after all, does not live in a vacuum, and all sorts of influences—the arrival of another child, new vocational interests, increasing maturity— may well bring about subtle yet important changes in her relationship to the child. Most important of all, however, are the changes that stem from the relationship itself: an overanxious mother sees her new baby prosper, gains confidence, and treats him with ever-increasing assurance. Or, alternatively, a mother encounters a persistent feeding difficulty in the baby, fails to resolve it, and as a result loses her initial equanimity and becomes tense and fearful with him (and if that, in turn, then makes the feeding problem even worse, one is left with a vicious spiral of the kind that can only be resolved by some drastic outside intervention and which clearly shows, moreover, the difficulty of disentangling cause and effect when confronted by the end result).

These examples are of short-term changes, and it may well be that long-term changes are even more marked. Of course there remains a core of consistency which would normally outweigh by far the fluctuations. Nevertheless, to conceive of parents as utterly static in the child's psychological life is likely to distort the picture grossly. A child's development always takes place within a context of contemporaneous events, the most important of which result from the parents' activities. And it appears that these activities need to be reassessed periodically if one is to understand the child's developmental course.

The relationship as an interaction. It is because the context of the child's development is always changing that one cannot predict later behavior on the basis of earlier events. According to explanations based on the critical-period model, early events have such great impact that one need not take anything else into account. This view, it appears, is too simpleminded: a baby does not become a different kind of adult for being bottle- rather than breast-fed, for being weaned early rather than late, for encountering one kind of attitude rather than another at some particular time. Single events rarely cause a major restructuring of the child's personality: they occur in the context of a continuous interaction with the environment, which itself is not static and which may modify, strengthen, or weaken the consequences of what has happened already. Only very rarely will a particular experience have such massive effects that it overrides all else, producing identical consequences for any child—at least, very rarely in human development, for it is likely that the effects of early experience seen in animal experiments are in most cases largely due to the enormous scale of the experiences involved. It seems improbable that anything comparable to the traumata commonly employed in psychological experiments with mice, rats, and dogs would be encountered by human children. What follows from the normal range of experience depends very much on the effects produced by the child's altered condition on the parents and, in turn, by the way in which that parental reaction impinges on the child. This applies even to such comparatively gross factors as minimal brain damage: in one family, its effects may be modified and normalized; in another, they may be exaggerated and become the starting point of considerable behavior problems. The labels parents attach to particular behavior patterns often reflect this: thus one set of parents may see a grossly inactive baby as "placid" and happily accept him as that, while another set might see the same child as irritatingly "lazy" and accordingly try to force him to behave differently. Knowing that a child has, for instance, minimal brain damage, without knowing the nature of his environment, will not tell us how he will develop.

So we need a "transactional model" rather than a critical-period model if we are to understand the course of child development—transactional in the sense that we recognize the constant and progressive mutual modifications of parent and child at all stages of growth. The fact that a child is weaned early (or undergoes a period of separation, or has minimal brain damage, or loses a parent through death) will not by itself tell one about the eventual outcome. The child is too much part of his immediate social environment to justify disregard of the effect that he has on his caregivers and of the effect that their reaction in turn will have on him. Both parents and child operate within a system of mutuality where the behavior of one produces effects on the other that in turn modify the behavior of the first. One has to consider the whole network of interacting influences, not, as the critical-period model attempts to do, skip all but the first and last link.

CONCLUSIONS

The two approaches to the study of the mother and child relationship we have discussed so far—that based on physical care and that dealing with attitudes—each originally hoped to reveal the major determinants of children's personality development; neither, however, has succeeded in this task. As a result, two changes have taken place in recent years in the way in which the mother-child relationship is being studied. In the first place, instead of searching for the long-term consequences of early family experiences, a switch has taken place to the study of immediate effects. The problem of bridging the gap between early experience and later personality has for the time been shelved, and questions are being asked instead about what is indeed the logically prior problem: whether and in what way infants of various ages are affected by specified environmental happenings. Let us first (so the reasoning goes) consider the immediate impact of mother and child on one another before we try to stipulate the relationship between infant experience and adult behavior.

The second change follows on the first. Once mother-infant interactions came to be studied in detail, it became clear that we needed to reshape radically our ideas about socialization—about how children are integrated into a social world. Formerly, socialization had been seen as a kind of "clay molding." The child, it was thought, came into the world as a formless, inert blob of clay which was then molded by parents, teachers, society, or whatever other forces he happened to come into contact with, and the shape that he eventually assumed was therefore entirely due to the characteristics others had decided to implant in him. This view, we now know, is misleading: probably more than any other single factor, it is responsible for past failures to understand the socialization process. As detailed examinations of mother-infant interactions show, from the beginning the baby is active, not passive; his behavior is organized, not "absent"; and even to the earliest social interactions he brings certain characteristics that will affect the behavior of other people toward him. A mother's task is thus not to create something out of nothing but rather to dovetail her behavior to that of the infant's. Before continuing with this account of mothering, we must therefore examine the nature of the infant's psychological organization in greater detail, for mothering can, after all, only be understood in relation to the kind of being that is to be mothered.

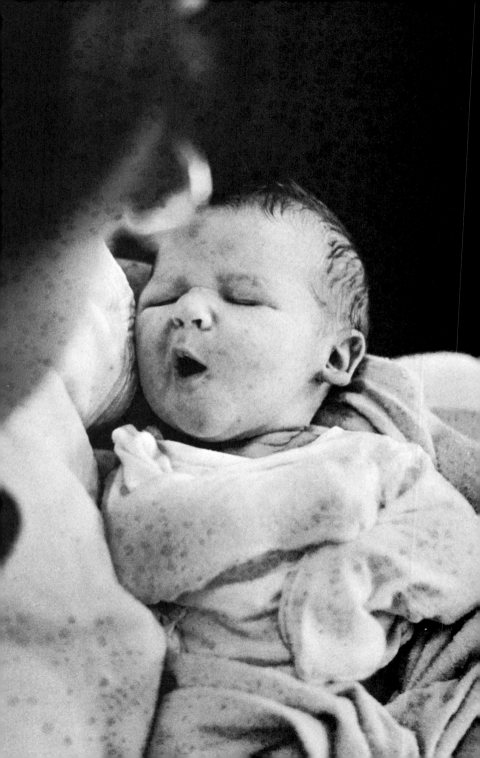

3 / The Organization of Infant Behavior

For a long time it was thought that in the early weeks of life a baby's senses were not yet capable of taking in any information from the outside world, so that to all intents and purposes he was blind and deaf. Unable to move much either, he seemed a picture of psychological incompetence, of confusion and disorganization. Only the regularity of his experience, provided principally by his parents, was thought to bring order to the baby's mind. Until that was achieved, all he could do was feed and sleep.

In the last decade or two a great deal has been learned about infant behavior which shows that all this is quite wrong. Thanks largely to a number of new techniques for measuring previously elusive aspects of infant behavior, data have accumulated which show that there *is* organization and greater competence than was previously thought, right from the very beginning. To illustrate, let us look at the view that babies can do little except feed and sleep. Even if that were true, analysis of just feeding and sleeping soon reveals how complex psychological functioning is, even at birth. So, in order to appreciate the baby's own organization, let us turn to these two functions.

SLEEPING AND WAKING

It is only fairly recently that psychologists have discovered what goes on in sleeping and waking states. Previously, only the amount of a baby's sleep was of interest. Even here we find a change of opinion. The old notion that a young baby spent most of his time asleep was, we now know, inaccurate. For instance, one study by A. H. Parmelee and his colleagues has revealed that sleep averages 16 hours 20 minutes in the first week and only 14 hours 50 minutes by the sixteenth week. There were considerable differences between individual babies, but it does seem that most are awake—and free to devote their time to other things—for about one third of each day, even in the period just following birth.[1]

The more striking changes of the early weeks, however, occur not so much in the duration of daily sleep as in the length of the individual periods of sleep and wakefulness and in their distribution around the clock. A newborn tends to sleep for many short periods, randomly distributed throughout the day and interspersed with even shorter periods of wakefulness. With age, both sleep and waking quickly assume a much more regular form: the periods become longer, they are less randomly distributed, and soon become organized in a diurnal pattern. Parmelee found a slight change in the day-night distribution already present in the first week of life; then the subjects slept an average of 7 hours 45 minutes during the day and 8 hours 20 minutes at night. By sixteen weeks, these figures had become 4 hours 35 minutes and almost 10 hours. Establishing a rhythm of diurnal waking and nocturnal sleep is in fact one of the more important developments in early infancy—it makes the baby so much easier to live with! It also illustrates how the baby's own internal pattern comes to be influenced by environmental pressures.

Two kinds of sleep.   Neither sleeping nor waking represents a distinct, homogeneous state. For both adults and children (and, for that matter, for many animal species) there are two quite distinct phases of sleep, active and quiescent. This distinction was originally founded on body movements and bursts of rapid eye movements (REMs), but has since been confirmed by physiological measures of brain waves, heartrate, and breathing. However, since the REMs provide the most notable criterion, the two phases have come to be known as REM and no-REM sleep.

These two phases can be detected from the beginning. E. Aserinsky and N. Kleitman, in a pioneering study of neonatal sleep back in 1955,[2] observed a two-phase cycle of movement which lasted on average about 50 minutes. They noted that for about 20 to 25 minutes of this cycle a newborn remained quiet and almost motionless; for the remainder of the cycle there were both little muscle movements and larger limb movements, regularly accompanied by observable REMs and fluttering eyelids. An adult REM-no-REM cycle takes about 90 minutes, but during the first year of life there is little deviation from 50 minutes, regardless of time of day or interval since the last feed. It is thus clear that sleep adheres to the newborn's own definite, internally regulated rhythm. Periods of sleeping and wakefulness are controlled by a pretty accurate internal "clock."

The components of the sleep cycle, however, do show a marked change in the course of the early months of life. In the newborn, REM sleep accounts for over half of total sleep, and it seems that in the fetus it approaches 100 percent. The change is particularly marked in the first three months, at the end of which time no-REM is almost double REM sleep. In fact between birth and adulthood REM sleep diminishes by approximately 80 percent, while no-REM sleep decreases by only a quarter. Thus both the amount and the ratio of REM sleep diminish with increasing age.

Why is REM sleep so prevalent early on? What is its function? One (admittedly speculative) answer is that the considerable increase in nerve-cell activity, and blood flow in the brain that accompanies it, may be essential for the normal growth of brain tissue. The fetus, shielded by the womb, and the young baby, still relatively helpless, get little or no environmental stimulation; REM sleep may serve as a built-in self-stimulation system that periodically provides activity and so helps to prepare the brain for dealing with "real" stimulation. Once this real stimulation is provided, either by the baby's own activity or through the mother's initiative, REM sleep is no longer so vital. Maternal stimulation has come to take over from REM-type stimulation.

The concept of "state." As with sleep, so with wakefulness: here too a number of qualitatively distinct states have been distinguished. There has been much debate about how many there are, just how they may be identified, and whether there really are separate states rather than a continuum of sleep to wakefulness. The details of all this need not concern us here: let it suffice that there are now a number of scales on which it is possible to classify an infant's state at any particular moment and thus to relate it to how he responds to external stimulation.

The concept of state has become a most useful tool in attempts to bring order to the variability of infant behavior. States are generally taken to represent sustained levels of brain activity, showing themselves in such diverse forms as deep sleep, alert inactivity, high excitability, and so on. They tend to occur spontaneously, being internally regulated by mechanisms about which little is so far known, and yet are by no means impervious to external influences. Given a constant level of stimulation, they may be of quite regular lengths, recurring cyclically and often in predictable sequences.

The most commonly used classification of states is that of H. F. R. Prechtl and D. J. Beintema,[3] which consists of five clusters:

> *State 1* (deep or "regular" sleep): eyes closed, regular breathing, no movements except startles
> *State 2* (active or "irregular" sleep): eyes closed, irregular breathing, small muscular twitches, no large movements
> *State 3* (alert inactivity): eyes open, no large movements
> *State 4* (alert activity): eyes open, diffuse movement, irregular breathing
> *State 5* (crying): eyes partly or wholly closed, vigorous diffuse movement, and cries

Various physiological indices like heartrate and the electrical activity of the brain or the muscles may also be added to these definitions to give each one its distinctive flavor.

As far as we are concerned, the concept of state is important because it illustrates two essential characteristics of infant behavior—its *spontaneity* and its *periodicity*. As to spontaneity, we can see here that the infant is by no means inert and passive, stirred into action only by outside stimulation. On the contrary, it appears that there are internal forces that regulate much of his behavior and account for changes in his activity. An external stimulus always impinges on an *active* creature, whatever the age, and in the early months of life in particular the infant's state plays a large part in determining his responsiveness to the outside world. In due course he becomes less constrained by these inner forces; but in the first six months especially the manner, the speed, and the intensity with which he responds to a given stimulus—indeed, whether he responds at all—depend very much on the particular state he happens to be in at the time of the encounter. It is apparent that "state reading" will be an essential part of successfully mothering the young baby.

The second characteristic, periodicity, is vividly illustrated by the cyclic alternation of states. There are, it appears, certain fixed rhythms that underlie the spontaneously occurring state changes. Some center in the brain is almost certainly responsible for this regularity, for it has been shown that brain injury may destroy or impair the cycle. This condition may rectify itself in due course; but it does seem that "neurologically deviant" children do tend to show abnormalities in state transitions. This is described by John Hutt and his colleagues, who write that "at-risk" babies tend to be characterized by prolonged irregular sleep and brief regular sleep.[4] So there are a number of indications that the baby has internal regulating devices within his brain which ensure that states keep changing. These changes are not haphazard, though—a fact that helps to make him a rather more predictable creature to his caregivers.

SUCKING

Freud's interest in oral behavior lay primarily in its role in personality development. But more recently oral behavior, and particularly sucking, has been studied in a much more detailed, analytic manner and primarily for its own sake. Sucking is, after all, the first essential way in which the baby comes into contact with the outside world. How he sucks should therefore tell us something about infant behavior and its part in social interaction.

Sucking is an inborn response, whose biological usefulness need hardly be stressed. It is functional from birth, but does need some priming—vigorous sucking may not be established for two or three days following birth. During this period the baby must adapt himself to the shape of the particular maternal breast or bottle with which he comes into contact. Both the need to do this and his ability to do it show that the sucking reflex is by no means as reflexive as, say, the knee jerk. It is a highly complex, internally organized response; but it is also variable and able to take into account the nature of the external stimulation it encounters. No wonder Piaget called it "the beginnings of psychology." No wonder, too—given the mutual adaptation both mother and baby require—that M. P. Middlemore referred to them as "the nursing couple."

Sucking is, in fact, just one component of the total feeding act, which is made up of the rooting reflex (turning of the head toward the nipple), opening the mouth and grasping the nipple with the lips, sucking, and swallowing. To function properly, these activities, together with breathing, must all be very finely integrated in sequence, so that together they make up a coordinated system that can deal effectively with a far from constant environment (the breast or bottle shifts, the flow of milk varies, the temperature changes, and so on). Such coordination is there from birth: it would serve the newborn ill if he had to acquire it, and it would make the mother's task even more complex if she had somehow to teach it.

The periodicity of sucking. How far complex organization is part of the newborn's nature becomes even clearer when we turn to examine the make-up of sucking itself. Sucking is an example of a "high-frequency micro-rhythm"—that is, an apparently simple activity which is in fact organized in complex time sequences. This is especially apparent for "nonnutritive sucking," for example sucking a pacifier. It then appears as a burst-pause pattern, with the number of sucks per burst ranging from about 5 to 20 and the pauses lasting between 4 and 15 seconds. The precise amounts depend on such factors as the infant's state, whether sucking is spontaneous or elicited, and on various individual characteristics. Mostly, however, it takes place at a fairly constant rate of 2 sucks per second. There is thus a definite temporal pattern which—as in the case of the sleep-waking cycle—is primarily regulated by an inborn mechanism in the brain. Infants with congenital mouth defects show no disturbance in the cycle; in some brain-injured infants, on the other hand, the burst-pause rhythm shows marked irregularities.

Once again the regular periodicity of infant behavior is clear. The variation in average frequency of sucks from burst to burst tends to be extremely small for any one infant, and slight even between individuals. Peter Wolff showed that nonnutritive sucking was so regular for each particular infant that one could work out pretty accurately when each new burst was likely to start and how long it would last.[5] He also found that, when the pacifier was removed right after the beginning of a burst of sucking, an infant generally continued to make empty mouthing movements up to the usual number of sucks per burst. Once a burst has started, therefore, it seems to run its course regardless. Such remarkable invariance suggests a very stable mechanism from birth for regulating the sucking response.

The adaptability of sucking. Sucking is not, however, by any means impervious to external influence. For one thing, the sucking rate can be affected by the rate of milk flow, the size, contour, and compressibility of the nipple, and the type of nutrient. As early as the first day of life, infants have been found to show different responses to two types of nutrient (a milk formula and 5 percent corn syrup). But how far a baby gains control over sucking is illustrated even more strikingly by experiments which show that three-month-olds can learn to suck vigorously to illuminate a picture in a darkened room, or merely to bring one back into focus. This same ability to adapt is shown by experiments in which the structure of individual sucks has been modified. This structure may be described in terms of two components: expression (positive sucking) and suctioning (negative sucking). If it is arranged that only one of these will deliver the milk, then the infant can adapt his sucking action in such a way that the other gradually diminishes and even drops out. The marvelous adaptability of sucking is only matched by the impressive intricacy of its innate constitution.

The periodicity of sucking is clear, and so also is its spontaneity. It is not something that happens only when the baby bumps into something to suck: even very small babies will grope and actively search for the nipple. Spontaneous mouthing, moreover, is also quite usual, especially *after* feeding, which shows that the function of oral behavior is not just to reduce hunger tension. A very detailed description of mouthing has been provided by Peter Wolff, who shows that this sort of early spontaneous behavior is very dependent on the infant's state at the time.[6] He shows as well that the same rhythmical burst-pause pattern appears in spontaneous mouthing as in sucking a pacifier. Nutritive sucking, on the other hand, does not show this pattern in as clear a form. Particularly at the beginning of a feed it is generally organized in a continuous stream, proceeding for several minutes without interruption before it too breaks up into the burst-pause routine. It seems likely that the rate of milk flow is what governs this: breastfeedings begin with continuous sucking, followed by the burst-pause pattern. When the baby is moved to the other breast, he begins once more with continuous sucking. Pauses are evidently due to milk depletion rather than to fatigue. Whether bottle feeding is characterized by a burst-pause pattern or not depends entirely on milk flow and thus on the type of nipple employed. In general, however, nutritive sucking contains longer bursts and shorter pauses, and the rate of sucking is about half as brisk as in nonnutritive sucking.

The central mechanism that regulates the sucking does not by any means function in isolation but is modulated by changes both inside and outside the infant. Sucking varies with state, as we have seen, and it varies with external change as well: cutting off the milk supply for a period will have an infant rapidly switching from nutritive to nonnutritive sucking and back again.

Thus a detailed analysis of sucking shows us how complex it really is. It is by no means a simple stereotyped activity, passively elicited by the mother's stimulation. It is, rather, precisely regulated—and highly sophisticated, not only in its internal organization but also in the way it is synchronized with other physiological functions like swallowing and breathing. The sucking rhythm is intimately linked to these and controls them: for instance, at the beginning of nutritional feeding the breathing rate will adjust. It is this total and various system, organized from birth, that must then become linked in feeding to the mother's response system—must become synchronized between the two as well as just within the baby.

THE ORGANIZATION OF PERCEPTION

But babies do *not* spend all their time feeding and sleeping. As we saw, even the newborn is awake for a third of his day, and soon much of this time is spent attending to events around him.

It used to be thought that a baby was initially conscious only of internal sensations such as pain, cold, and hunger, that he was quite unaware of the outside world. This notion was based on the lack of any obvious signs of awareness, for when someone can neither talk about nor act on his sensations it is tempting simply to conclude that he has none. Now that there are new ways to explore the baby's perceptual world, we know this is not the case: from birth on, most sense organs can function, albeit in a limited manner, and soon a baby is able to build up a stock of information about the external world.

Visual responsiveness. Take looking as an example. In an immature way, most visual capacities are already present at birth, and they quickly mature in the following weeks. From the beginning, the baby's pupil will contract in intense light, enabling him to control the amount of light to which he is exposed. Another defensive reflex, the blink at an approaching object, appears from about two months. Following a moving object, jerky and inefficient at first, becomes much smoother and more successful within the later months; a four- or five-month-old can follow a moving person without difficulty. Coordination of the two eyes is at first somewhat poor; for instance, the baby can focus on an object only at about eight inches distance—anything nearer or further tends to be blurred. Fortunately the most important things, particularly the mother's face, frequently appear at this distance; moreover, the range of focusing quickly increases, reaching adult standards by the fourth month.

The baby can see a good deal; he also spontaneously looks. As with sucking, so with looking: he does not lie passively until something happens to impinge on his vision, but spends his time actively searching for something to look at. Such spontaneity, it is true, depends a great deal on the infant's state; when he is overexcited and crying, he is too bombarded by stimulation from within to be free to attend to the outside world. But when he is actively alert he will keep scanning a blank environment until something is produced that he can settle his attention on.

Eye movements are yet another "random" activity which, on closer inspection, turns out to be orderly and based on regular periodicities. The continuous, tiny, step-wise movements recorded in adults' eyes and known as "saccades" are already evident in newborns and appear in bursts of highly regular frequency. Here too there is evidence of a brain mechanism responsible for periodicity; just as with sucking, the much more complex and sophisticated manifestations that appear later are built up developmentally on the basis of micro-rhythms already evident at birth.

But the organization of a newborn's eye movements is anything but simple. In the first place, the saccades of the two eyes are already completely synchronized. Second, from the beginning there is some coordination between the movements of the eyes and of the head and, while this is rather imperfect at first, the basis for tracking moving objects (which appears clearly in the later weeks) is already provided at birth. Again, just as sucking is innately coordinated with rooting, swallowing, and breathing, so movements of the eyes are integrated from the beginning with movements of the head.

With experience such coordination may become more perfect; yet its presence not only in newborns but also in blind babies clearly indicates that it is inborn. Visual behavior, in other words, is based on mechanisms that are just as evident before the baby has developed a relationship to the environment as they are in maturity.

What *does* change is the proportion of time that the infant can spend in a state of visual alertness; as a result of this change, he can increasingly use his visual mechanisms actively to select objects around him and explore them purposively. It is then that another crucial characteristic of infant perception becomes particularly evident: its selectivity. The baby already has certain preferences as to what he finds most interesting to look at. Since these can be demonstrated as early as the first week of life, the newborn must have a number of built-in selective mechanisms which ensure that he pays more attention to some parts of his surroundings than to others.

Our knowledge about these mechanisms owes much to the perfection of the "visual preference technique" by R. L. Fantz. This technique circumvents the problem that the infant can neither move nor speak by measuring instead how much he looks at each of two stimuli presented simultaneously in a specially designed apparatus. If he consistently pays more attention to one than the other, he is said not only to be able to distinguish the pair but also to "prefer" that one.

While this method does have certain drawbacks (for example, it does not follow from a lack of visual preference that the infant *cannot* make a distinction), it has made possible the discovery that babies are much more likely to pay attention to certain features than to others. When, for example, Fantz paired patterned surfaces (such as horizontal stripes or concentric circles) with highly colored but plain ones, infants attended far more to the patterns. Similarly, they attend to complexity (that is, to things which contain a diversity of distinguishable parts), to movement, and to three-dimensionality. There are two points to be made about these preferences. In the first place, they again show that the infant is active. From the beginning of life, he is able to regulate what he takes in by selective attention. Given the choice, he will seek out those features of his surroundings to which, by virtue of his physical make-up, he is most sensitive. And the second point is that if we were to design an object that would contain all these features and thus be maximally attention-worthy, we would end up with a human being. This is indeed the conclusion that one may reach from the abundant research done in recent years using human faces as stimuli. Whether one presents live faces or representations, whether the faces are schematic or real, two-dimensional or three-dimensional, appear in the flesh or on film—in every case, infants are fascinated by them, often to the exclusion of all else. The eyes in particular are an important source of attraction: studies of the baby's smile have shown that in the first few months he will smile immediately at a mask bearing nothing but a pair of eyelike dots. A mouth or any other single feature will not do. It is as though the infant is biologically "set" to be triggered by certain quite specific yet primitive stimuli—stimuli found on other human beings. And one can, of course, readily understand that it would be biologically useful for a baby to be prepared from the very beginning for interaction with other human beings.

Responsiveness to sound. Such preadaptation can also be found in babies' perception of sound. Again, the discovery of new techniques has altered a previous impression of early incompetence. For example, by monitoring changes in heartrate or in sucking it has become possible to show that babies can differentiate sounds to an impressive degree. Within the first week of life, they can discriminate the loudness and pitch of sounds and, more controversially, locate where they are coming from. The precise degree of discrimination may depend on various factors in the experimental setting and especially on the infant's state, but often a newborn's ability can be shown to approach that of an adult—for instance, the minimum sound level he can respond to, when optimally alert, is almost the same as that for adults. The notion that a baby is at first functionally deaf can certainly be discounted.

Again, however, the sensory apparatus is selective, and again it appears particularly tuned to humanlike stimuli—speech sounds, in this case. In a study of infants between three and eight days of age, John Hutt obtained electrical recordings from muscles in response to a number of different noises and found that voices and voicelike sounds produced the greatest responses. All along, it appears, the infant is particularly responsive to the human voice, for he is differentially tuned to frequencies in the range of speech. "Social preadaptation" thus takes an auditory as well as a visual form.

CONCLUSIONS

In the last decade or two we have witnessed a switch from the study of the experience-giving parent to the study of the experiencing infant. A great deal has been learned about psychological abilities in the early months and years of life, and as a result our concept of the infant has changed drastically. Instead of regarding him as initially a psychological nonentity, as a being that only takes shape by virtue of the parental socializing practices he encounters, we have come to recognize that all along a baby's behavior shows order and organization, and that the buzzing confusion which William James once attributed to the infant's perceptual world lay not in him but in our own minds and recording techniques. Even the newborn is distinguished by certain orderly characteristics, and these need to be taken into account if one is to understand the mother's interaction with her baby. Due attention must be paid to the peculiarities of *both* partners.

The features of infant behavior which particularly matter for social interaction are its spontaneity, its periodicity, and its selectivity. Since it is spontaneous, the adult is not dealing with an inert, passive organism that he must stimulate into life. The task of the socializing parent is therefore not to create behavior out of nothing, but rather to synchronize with behavior that is already organized.

Periodicity is one way in which the spontaneous nature of the infant's behavior expresses itself; selectivity is another. The youngest baby will attend to and interact with his environment in a far from indiscriminate way. As we have seen, he will respond particularly to human characteristics, and in this way it is ensured that his social partners will assume a special significance for him from birth. In due course the basis of the baby's selective behavior changes, for eventually he will come to discriminate among other people on the basis of previous experience and will classify them according to their familiarity or unfamiliarity. This, however, requires an extended learning period, during which he becomes acquainted with his caregivers; until then, he attends to characteristics common to all human beings, who will accordingly be smiled at, cried for, visually followed, sucked, and clung to, and thus repeatedly challenged by him on his own initiative to engage in social exchange.

4/ Mothering as Stimulation

Given the infant's active striving to interact with his environment, what should that environment offer him? At its simplest, the answer could be *stimulation*. Development does not take place in a vacuum; it needs the active participation of those involved in the baby's care. They must structure the environment so as to maximize his opportunities for progressively more complex interactions. Parents must play, talk, handle, demonstrate, sing, rock, cuddle, and carry out all the other activities that so naturally make up most parents' repertoire.

DEVELOPMENT AND CHILD CARE

Not that the association between stimulation and developmental progress—seemingly so obvious now—has always been accepted. In this respect more than most, childrearing has been subject to violent swings of fashion, from a "leave well alone" policy at one extreme to a "the more the better" policy at the other. The first of these was given a cloak of intellectual respectability in 1928 by Arnold Gesell, with his concept of maturation as the principal determinant of early development.[1] Gesell believed that the early years showed an orderly, predetermined unfolding of inherent capacities, affected only minimally by an infant's encounters with the particular environment in which he was reared. He was convinced that development could not be accelerated by any form of stimulation, and indeed expressed gratitude that infancy was not characterized by what he called "flaccid malleability," for babies might then succumb too easily to misguided management. Gesell, it seems, did not have a particularly sanguine view of parents.

The "leave well alone" policy of child care was very influential during the 1930s and 1940s. It was based on the assumption that a child's natural environment was generally quite adequate to nourish early development, in that it provided the setting in which forces inherent in the child would inevitably unfold. We now know that this assumption is wrong. A great deal of evidence indicates that development does not take place in a vacuum; it requires an environment that stimulates the baby to realize his potential.

And so the second view of childrearing, "the more the better," came into being. The evidence on which this is based comes from various well-known studies which have shown that developmental progress does not necessarily take a regular, steadily accelerating course irrespective of happenings in the outside world but that, quite on the contrary, a child's experiences might well produce wide fluctuations in his intellectual capabilities. Much of this material has been discussed in relation to the IQ debate and the justice of putting children into rigidly separate educational categories on the basis of earlier tests. Most dramatically, however, the evidence emerged from studies of deprived infants such as those in the Lebanon creche mentioned in Chapter Two.[2] In the appalling conditions described there, an apparently normal child could become to all intents and purposes a mental defective manufactured by society.

A rather less dramatic but much more common indication of the same trend is found among the "culturally deprived" or "disadvantaged." Children coming from underprivileged homes, where they receive little intellectual stimulation, few opportunities to satisfy their curiosity, and limited guidance in exploring the world, fall behind the developmental norm for their age group. This trend has been said to begin in the third year of life, when linguistic skills should be developing, and has indeed been largely ascribed to the verbal impoverishment of such children's homes. More recently, however, several reports have suggested that, given the right assessment techniques, one can find the beginnings of the downward trend as early as the first year.

The detrimental effects of adverse conditions have been clearly demonstrated. A young child needs to be stimulated by those around him, and so it follows, it was thought, that we have a remedial tool available for those who have not been stimulated enough: we can provide them with a bit extra over and above what they would otherwise get. And the more the better: thus one study attempted to rectify some institutionalized infants' lack of interpersonal experience by giving them a daily dose of tactile stimulation—ten minutes of skin stroking in the morning and another ten in the afternoon, provided at a fixed time five days a week for several weeks by students specially hired for the job (and referred to in the report on the study as "handlers"). The results of this particular experiment—like those of a companion study in which extra verbal stimulation was provided by an adult standing next to each baby's crib and counting aloud for ten minutes on end—showed, not surprisingly, none of the improvement in developmental test scores that the investigator had hoped for. What a very good example in fact of the "blob of clay" conception of the infant, on whom stimulation is imposed arbitrarily, without regard for his state and condition, his willingness at the time to engage in social interaction, his own ability to determine its nature, or the effect that any one "stimulation episode" might be seen to produce! In short, the "problem of the match," as J. McV. Hunt once called it, is discounted. However well motivated the craze for early perceptual enrichment may have been, the forms it took (from the maternity hospital that decided to provide all its newborns with striped sheets instead of plain ones onward) tended only too often to disregard the nature of the creature being enriched.

So early socialization is neither a matter of leave well alone nor of the more the better. The first may result in neglect and failure to use a child's potential; the second involves arbitrarily imposed experiences that may be unrelated to the child's ability to assimilate them. We therefore need a third view of socialization, which sees both adult and child as actively involved together. An infant may need stimulation, but its amount, kind, and timing must be closely related to his own psychological organization.

STATE AND RESPONSIVENESS TO STIMULATION

A one-to-one correspondence between a mother's stimulation and her baby's response simply does not exist. How readily that response is called forth, its nature, its frequency, and how long it is maintained depend above all on an infant's particular state at the time. The same stimulus may well elicit quite different responses on different occasions—an observation which previously seemed merely to prove that a baby is a disorganized being in whom no orderly relationships with his environment could be discerned. However, by taking state into account it becomes possible to understand a lot of such variation in his behavior. State, in other words, mediates and filters stimulation.

State and sensitivity. Let us illustrate the relationship between state and responsiveness with some observations reported by Peter Wolff.[3] Taking twelve newborns as subjects, Wolff examined what difference their state made to how much more (or less) active they became when exposed to pain, touch, or sound. He found that there was indeed considerable variation from state to state in the infants' sensitivity, but that this depended on the kind of stimulation. In the case of touch and sound there was little responsiveness in regular sleep, most response somewhere between irregular sleep and waking activity, and diminished responsiveness during crying. Thus there appeared to be relative insensitivity at both ends of the state continuum. On the other hand, pain produced most response during the two sleep states but less during waking activity, when touch and sound reach their zenith. So the relationship between responsiveness and state varied according to the sense involved.

This point also emerges from a study carried out by Lamper and Eisdorfer.[4] Forty babies were examined on each of their first three days of life. The stimuli were auditory (two tones of different loudness), tactual (a cotton ball applied to the nasal septum), and cold (a stainless steel instrument immersed in ice water and then held against the hapless baby's inner thigh). The response to sound and touch, it was found, depended on the infants' state rather as Wolff had shown. In the case of cold, on the other hand, which consistently and hardly surprisingly elicited the most intense response, the effects of state were simply overridden. It seems that responses to more compelling stimuli may depend less on the infant's internal condition than do those within the more usual range of experience.

When a pediatrician examines a baby's neurological condition, he proceeds by working through the newborn's repertoire of reflexes. But to carry out such an examination without taking into account the infant's state at the time is likely to produce a grossly misleading picture. Some reflexes, such as the knee jerk (the "monosynaptic" group), are differently influenced by state than others ("polysynaptic" reflexes such as the palmar grasp response by which the infant grasps a finger or object that touches his palm). The former are at their maximum when the infant is awake but quiet, and fairly marked during regular sleep; but in irregular sleep they are absent or weak. The latter, on the other hand, are elicited most easily in irregular sleep, are less obvious in the quiet but awake infant, and virtually absent in regular sleep. Add to that the observation that reflexes to noxious stimuli may be obtained quite irrespective of state, and it becomes apparent that the relationship between responsiveness and state is indeed a complex one. Anyone who has ever tried to get a smile out of a fretting baby knows that a baby's internal condition affects responsiveness; what is not so apparent is that different responses are affected quite differently.

State and the type of response. The influence of state is clear not only in the likelihood of a response but also in its nature. A further observation by Wolff makes this point: the sound that produced a smile during irregular sleep or drowsiness evoked not smiling but the Moro (or startle) reflex during regular sleep.[5] And, similarly, Pat-a-Cake games that elicit smiling when a baby is content will provoke crying when he is active or fussy. A silent, nodding head may call forth intent interest when he is alert, but crying (even to the mother's face) when he is restless. State thus alters the significance the stimulus has for the infant. Anneliese Korner recorded the responses of newborns to the whir of a camera, and found activation (startle, increased motion, grimaces, even crying) if the baby was in a quiet state, but quieting (decreased crying, less activity, scanning as if to locate the sound) if he was highly aroused.[6] Thus a response may assume a quite different direction, depending on the infant's state. A touch may produce movement in a baby alertly inactive but will quiet him if he is crying.

All this shows just how important state reading is when dealing with an infant. An adult generally wants to know roughly what response he will produce with any particular form of stimulation. When he picks up the baby, boisterously swings him through the air, and bounces him up and down, he does so in the belief that the baby will respond by gurgling with delight. Whether that happens, though, depends entirely on how sensitively he read the baby's initial state, for under some conditions that treatment will produce screams of protest and howls of rage. Again we see the dangers of arbitrarily imposed stimulation; a baby's response is not only determined by the adult but also by the baby himself.

Not that one needs to teach mothers this point, for most will quite naturally act in an appropriate manner. David Levy observed mothers in a maternity hospital when their infants were brought to them for feeding.[7] In such a more or less standard situation he found a considerable range of different responses, determined primarily by the mother's awareness of her baby's state. How she greeted him, how she handled him, and the speed with which she offered the breast or bottle could all be related to how she perceived his readiness for these forms of stimulation. A mother's sensitivity to her baby's state will thus determine what kind of stimulation she provides.

THE INFLUENCE OF STIMULATION ON STATE

So far we have discussed the effects of the infant's state on his response to stimulation. The relationship is, however, a two-way affair, for the baby's state may well change in turn as a result of interaction with another person.

Although states may fluctuate spontaneously according to internal regulating devices, they are affected by the outside world as well. Changes can be brought about by dressing or undressing, by a rise or fall in temperature, or by variations in noise or ambient light. When state ought as far as possible to be held constant, such as during the pediatrician's examination, it is important to attend to such factors.

Maternal handling and state changes. Changes brought about by the adult may be either arousing or quieting. The most potent arousers generally involve a complex of varied stimulation. Undressing the baby, for instance, entails touch and movement as well as changes in position and temperature. For mothers, however, the problem is rarely a matter of arousing their baby, but usually of reducing an excessively high level of arousal.

A study by Anneliese Korner and Rose Grobstein looks at one answer to this problem.[8] Crying babies were picked up and put to the shoulder, and the effect of that was compared with either merely propping them up to a sitting position or leaving them in their cribs without any intervention at all. The babies picked up were not only more likely to stop crying but would also open their eyes and look about. The difference was apparent for every one of them, though some quieted down more quickly than others.

Picking up is, of course, one of the commonest maternal ministrations. But just what is it about picking up that produces the effect? Is it the body contact between mother and baby? Is it the upright position? Or is it the "vestibular stimulation" produced by the act of moving him? In a further study Korner and Evelyn Thoman established that vestibular stimulation, the experience of being moved about, was the crucial ingredient that effectively brought about soothing and visual alertness.[9] This is particularly interesting in view of the fact that so many people regard bodily contact as the very essence of early mothering. For instance Margaret Ribble, writing in 1944, believed that to be stroked, cuddled, and fondled was indeed a basic precondition for psychological growth, and that not to experience close tactual contact with the body of the mother could have serious consequences. But it now looks as though, for very young babies at least, the mother's movement is far more effective at making a crying infant calm, alert, and attentive to his surroundings.

Korner's studies also illustrate that, paradoxically, one of the best ways for a mother to provide stimulation is to soothe her baby. By providing him with this kind of comfort she reduces his level of arousal, ensuring that he is not bombarded by internal stimuli and is therefore free to attend to his external environment. Much of early mothering, in other words, is a matter of modulating the baby's state, warding off stimulation as well as providing it, protecting against excessive doses as well as supplying extra stimuli. The interaction of mother and baby is often treated as a purely emotional affair; yet it appears that certain quite specific aspects also have cognitive—intellectual—implications, in that they enable the baby to attain a level of attentiveness at which he can begin to explore his surroundings and perceptually (later on also manipulatively) familiarize himself with the environment. It may well be that lack of this modulating influence of mothering is one of the crucial elements that retards institutionalized infants. When caregivers do not have the time or sensitivity to help a baby to reach a state in which he can maximally profit from encounters with his world, even the richest environment will fail to get through to him. In the end it is the personal attention involved in picking up rather than a great range of impersonal toys that speeds developmental progress.

Continuous stimulation. If one wants merely to quiet an infant, it appears that the most effective means is to provide some form of continuous and monotonous stimulation. It has been found, for instance, that continuous sound reduces activity and soothes distressed babies particularly effectively, though just how effectively depends on the state of the infant at the beginning. The most dramatic effect is found during irregular sleep, which is almost always converted to regular sleep—generally within about a minute. If the baby is drowsy or softly crying the effect, though less dramatic, is still considerable. If he is crying vigorously, however, the sound produces a change in state only occasionally.

Yvonne Brackbill observed twenty-four newborns in four situations: with a metronome beating, a lullaby being sung, a recorded heartbeat being played, and in silence.[10] There was less crying and less activity, a lower and more regular heartrate, and less variable respiration when there was some sound than when there was none. In a later study she went on to contrast the behavior of one-month-olds with no sound, continuous sound, and intermittent sound.[11] Arousal was highest under intermittent and lowest under continuous stimulation. There was no crying at all with continuous sound, whereas with intermittent sound the infants spent about a quarter of the time crying.

There are indications that a similar effect can be obtained with other senses. It seems, for instance, that light might have a similar effect, though less compelling. Brackbill set out to see whether the different senses are in fact equivalent in this respect; she also wanted to establish whether stimulating a number of senses simultaneously would have a cumulative effect.[12] Accordingly, one-month-old infants were presented with four types of continuous stimulation: a tape-recorded heartbeat, ambient light, swaddling from neck to toes in strips of flannel, and a temperature of 31°C. Any one, two, or three, or all four, or none of these were provided simultaneously. Once again the results emphasized the soothing effects of continuous stimulation. They also showed, however, that the effect applied generally to all the senses: quiet sleep, for example, was increased not only by the heartbeat but equally by the ambient light, by the rise in temperature, and by the swaddling. Furthermore, the pacification effect *was* cumulative, increasing according to the number of continuous stimuli simultaneously presented. This held, however, only for the two extreme states (quiet sleep or crying); in the intermediate states the rate of pacification indices did not change as total stimulation increased.

Swaddling deserves a special comment, since it is so widely used among so-called primitive communities. In the West, childcare experts have generally discouraged it in the belief that an infant must be able to exercise his limbs if he is to put them eventually to full use. There is at least some room to doubt this idea: the infants of Hopi Indians, despite being firmly swaddled and bound to cradle boards for most of their first year, still begin to walk at the usual sort of age. What is far less doubtful, however, is the immediate effect of swaddling. According to Brackbill, the very act of swaddling frequently produced such a dramatic state change that a baby who was crying when the experimenter began to swaddle him had stopped crying by the time swaddling was completed. It seems that the crucial thing is the restraint involved rather than the constant touch or increased warmth, for infants who were free to move but were covered with tight clothing were not soothed.

Thus continuous stimulation brings about state changes, and always in a "downward" direction. It is, however, important to add two qualifications to this, both stemming from observations made again by Wolff.[13] In the first place, Wolff considers that the apparently regular no-REM sleep induced by a continuous sound is in fact not a "natural" sleep: he found that such spontaneous responses as startles and mouthing took on a rather different pattern under such conditions from that of normal sleep.

This is only a tentative finding, but Wolff believes that the availability of commercial devices claiming to facilitate sleep through monotonous sound makes it important to be aware of it. The second point is that, however powerful continuous stimulation may be in inducing and maintaining sleep, the inherent biological clock that regulates the duration of regular sleep periods cannot easily be altered. Wolff noted that, from the second week on, regular no-REM sleep periods rarely lasted beyond 21 minutes. When he then examined the length of regular sleep periods during continuous sound, he noted that they were never substantially prolonged beyond that 21 minutes—whether the sound was turned on at the beginning, the middle, or toward the end of the cycle. The infant's inherent organization was thus firmly setting limits to environmental manipulation.

INDIVIDUAL DIFFERENCES IN RESPONSE TO STIMULATION

The concept of state illustrates strikingly the extent to which an infant's response to stimulation is due to factors within him. A look at individual differences shows the same thing: different infants respond to the same experience in varying ways.

Patterns of individuality have been revealed in many sorts of infant behavior, but only in a very few cases have they been shown to persist in the long term. Individual differences emerge from just about every study of even the very youngest babies; what they mean, if they are not just chance fluctuations, is only too often obscure. Some differences, it is true, can be traced back to perinatal experiences: sedating the mother at birth, for instance, has been shown to have various effects on vision and feeding in the baby's second week. But the origins of others are less certain. In one longitudinal study A. Thomas and his colleagues have tried to sort out nine "intrinsic reaction patterns," including such characteristics as activity level, attention span, threshold of responsiveness, and distractibility.[14] They claim these to be stable characteristics that endure over long periods, and, though their assessment of the "patterns" was somewhat crude, their list does at least contain some useful suggestions.

Cuddliness. But whatever the origin of such patterns, and however stable, there is no doubt that some can make a considerable difference to the way an infant responds to his mother's stimulation. Take "cuddliness" as an example. In a longitudinal study extending over the first eighteen months, Peggy Emerson and I noticed that there were marked, stable differences in how much infants sought close, physical contact with their mothers.[15] A number of babies were found actively to resist and protest at being embraced, hugged and held tight, even when they were tired, frightened, or ill. These "noncuddlers" were much more active, restless, and intolerant of such physical restraints as being dressed or tucked into bed than the "cuddlers," who tended to be more placid, to sleep more, and to resort more to cuddly toys. The differences were evident from the early weeks on and appeared not to stem from the way in which a mother handled her baby. Some mothers were forced very much against their will to comfort their babies, when unwell, in ways quite unlike the close contact they thought "natural"—they had to distract them with a biscuit or bottle, walk or carry them around, and so on. It was not that the noncuddlers showed a lack of orientation to the mother: she was, as with other children, a "haven of safety" to them and when frightened (as by an approaching stranger) they too sought to get near her. But instead of getting close by cuddling up, they preferred just to keep in visual touch or else, for instance, to hold on to her skirt or hide their faces against her knee.

It appears that the right kind of maternal intervention differs considerably between the two groups. What is appropriate in one case is not necessarily so in the other, and each mother must therefore show considerable flexibility in adjusting to the peculiarities of her child. Clearly she has certain requirements of her own that she wishes to fulfill in the relationship, and a matching process must therefore take place in which the two mutually adjust to one another. This cannot happen if the mother rigidly insists on providing her child with contact he cannot assimilate. But most mothers, however surpised they may be initially by noncuddling, quickly adjust and find other ways of furthering the relationship. It is only when they are too inflexible, or interpret the baby's behavior as rejection, that trouble can arise from a mismatch.

Activity level. Noncuddling appears in fact to be a manifestation of a more basic characteristic of a child, namely his activity level, for essentially what a noncuddler objects to is not contact as such but rather the restraint involved in picking him up and holding him close. It has become clear that there are differences in activity level that appear very early on, remain stable, and seem to be of constitutional origin. What is important to us is that there are indications that activity level may profoundly modify the impact that stimulation has on an infant. This is particularly well illustrated by some observations made by Sibylle Escalona of a group of infants between the ages of four weeks and thirty-two weeks.[16] Inactive babies were found to explore more with sight and touch; hunger excited the active ones intensely; showing an object greatly alerted the inactive babies but the active ones not particularly; and minimal social stimulation (such as the mere sight of a person) had a pronounced effect on the active babies, whereas the inactive ones required something very much more intense (like handling) before they responded in the same way. This adds up to a clear indication of the different effects of the same experience on active or inactive babies. Even going to hospital, where there is so little stimulation and social attention, can affect infants to varying extents depending on how active they are. Inactive babies are much more likely to be adversely affected than more active ones—presumably because they are less likely to change position and hence see new things, and also because they don't stimulate themselves so much with the sensation of moving about. But perhaps most important, the more alert and active baby is much more likely to catch the eyes of whatever caregivers are available and so get at least some extra attention.

Perceptual sensitivity.   Rather more controversial is the question of differences in "perceptual sensitivity." Individual babies have different thresholds for perception—that is, some need louder sounds or brighter lights than others to get them to start responding. Differences of this sort could, as Escalona suggests, increase or decrease the impact that one and the same maternal treatment has on different babies, but the evidence that this happens remains sparse so far. Indeed, it is still uncertain whether infants can simply be typed as sensitive or insensitive, that is, whether these differences in threshold cut across all the senses. At the moment, there is evidence both for and against this possibility.

That some babies are more sensitive (especially to noise) than others may seem a plausible notion; but it remains for research to confirm this impression and to determine how consistent these differences are over time and situation. If babies do vary in this way, it would indicate once again that the caregiver role is very much influenced by a baby's own characteristics, and that mothering must be very flexible if his individuality is to be respected.

THE INFLUENCE OF AN INFANT'S AGE AND SEX ON THE MOTHER'S BEHAVIOR

That a mother feels herself challenged to respond differently to different sorts of infant behavior is seen most clearly in connection with her baby's age and sex. It is true that it is often difficult to tell what is cause and what is effect—whether the different kinds of treatment that, say, a one- and a three-month-old get are elicited by the infant or are arbitrarily imposed by the mother. From what we have seen so far of the couple's interaction, the second seems unlikely. More probably, there is a progressive mutual modification, in that changes in the baby's development alter the mother's behavior and that this in turn affects the baby. Neither partner is a *tabula rasa* at any point: the infant, as we have seen, is endowed from the beginning with some form of psychological organization that stimulates others to behave in certain ways, but the mother too is biased toward interacting in particular ways and has certain preconceptions about her child that will color what she does.

Age effects. It is obvious that mothers treat babies of different ages differently. To take but one example: Howard Moss found pronounced shifts in how mothers stimulated their infants at three weeks and at three months.[17] In particular, holding the baby decreased by over 30 percent in this period. On the other hand, an appreciable increase occurred in attending to the baby, in that mothers tended to devote more of their time with him to visual contact (usually face to face) than to touch. During the same period there was also a marked increase in affectionate behavior, such as smiling and talking. It may be, as Peter Wolff has suggested, that a mother does not really feel that she is a "person" to the baby until he becomes capable of prolonged eye contact with her. This, together with the emergence of the smile in the second month, may well be responsible for injecting far more warmth into the relationship—even though the mother may realize that the child is still quite indiscriminate in the way he bestows his own affections.

Whether all these changes in the mother's behavior are due to the maturation of the infant's behavior remains an open issue. Certainly the mother's growing experience and confidence should not be overlooked. Nor ought we forget mothers' beliefs about what is right for babies of different ages; a woman's expectations and interpretations at different developmental stages may play a powerful part in shaping her behavior. Realizing that much of the mother-infant relationship is determined by infant characteristics should not blind us to the fact that mothers too are not just reactive beings, for they bring their own needs and hopes and norms to the relationship. One need only think of the violent shock that can follow a handicapped child's failure to reach age norms to appreciate the force of maternal aspirations.

Sex effects. All that I have just said is likely to be even truer where sex is concerned. To what extent there are genetically determined differences in the behavior of the two sexes remains controversial. On the one hand, there are such suggestive findings as that female newborns show greater sensitivity to touch and to oral stimulation than males. On the other hand, there is a marked lack of agreement about many other sex differences which have at one time or another been suggested—even about the idea that girls tend to be maturationally ahead of boys. It does seem likely, however, that males and females tend to be treated differently from a very early age: few mothers ever see their baby as an "it." Michael Lewis noticed that three-month-old boys were stimulated more by physical means, like cuddling, while girls were stimulated more by visual or auditory means.[18] It is of course possible that, if boys are less sensitive to touch, their mothers might have to provide them with more contact to have an impact on them. But Moss found something else that makes the causal relationship look even more complex: at three weeks of age mothers were cuddling their babies when they cried, irrespective of their sex; at three months, however, they cuddled girls when they cried but not necessarily the boys. Perhaps, as Moss suggests, if boys are inherently more irritable, the mothers were discouraged by failure and gave up trying to pacify them.

It is dangerous to generalize too much about mothers' ideas about what behavior is appropriate to the sexes in infancy. What part these play depends largely on each mother's own personality, background, and culture. As well as that, such ideas may well change as the mother learns more about her baby, who will certainly exert his individuality from early on. Sheer physical appearance may count here: it is much more difficult to treat a bald-headed girl as feminine than one who begins life already well endowed with flowing locks. Whether these differences have long-term implications, however, is doubtful; even the baldest baby girl eventually grows hair.

TIMING OF STIMULATION

It has already become apparent that one cannot arbitrarily heap stimulation on a baby, for its effects depend greatly on what is currently going on within him. The timing of stimulation thus becomes all-important.

That the relation in time between stimulus and response is significant even in the early weeks has been well established by the many studies of conditioning in babies. If his smile or vocalization is predictably followed by a smile or some talking back from his mother, the baby smiles and vocalizes more often. He learns that by his behavior he can produce certain effects, that he can control specific happenings. He thus becomes aware of a link between his action and the outside world.

Contingency and effectance. Such awareness has mostly been treated in terms of specific "stimulus-response bonds." Through the prompt action of his caregivers, that is, the child learns that specific activities have "signal value": he cries, and his mother appears; he coos and gurgles, and the adults around him respond with delight. He thus finds out that crying and cooing each produce a particular effect and that he can employ one or the other to manipulate his environment in particular ways. But possibly this is only part of the lesson he learns; much more important, he may develop a general expectation that he can indeed affect his environment. A baby therefore develops an "effectance motive" as he acquires a general confidence that he can produce consequences—even in those instances where he has yet had no chance to see whether a particular act will be effective or not. To develop such a motive a child's actions must be consistently and promptly reinforced, and it is one of the mother's functions to make this possible. Depending on her ability to do so, the child will in due course learn a generalized expectation either of control or of helplessness.

A condition of helplessness is most clearly visible in the lifestyle of those children not given the opportunity to learn what can follow from their behavior. A deprived child, living in an impersonal institution where his care is in the hands of many different individuals, each one of whom must also look after a large number of other children, may well not learn the signal value of his behavior. Where personal attention is regulated by routine, where the clock determines the timing of care, an infant's behavior is followed neither consistently nor promptly by any appropriate consequences. He cries, but no one comes to investigate; he coos and gurgles, but others are too busy to respond. How can he then learn the communicative value of his behavior? He can only learn that he is "helpless." The quietness and apathy so strikingly characteristic of deprived babies may well be an expression of this feeling, for there is little point in signaling for attention when no one is likely to notice. It may be that much of the developmental retardation so usual with institutionalized infants reflects absence of motivation rather than genuine inability. The deprived infant is simply not motivated to exhibit his skills, for he has learned that their performance is greeted with indifference. In the absence of any social response, his skills atrophy.

The pleasures to be derived from "contingency awareness" have been vividly described by John Watson.[19] In an attempt to stimulate this awareness in early infancy, he supplied two-month-old babies with a mobile that they themselves were able to activate by means of a sideways head movement on a special pillow. The babies not only learned to activate the mobile but appeared to regard the experience with an excitement normally reserved for interactions with other people. Just as a mother can call forth vigorous smiles and cooing, so the contingent stimulation supplied by the mobiles produced animated laughing, smiling, and vocalizing. This, according to Watson, is The Game, for it is in gamelike social interactions that babies normally first become aware of the relationship between their behavior and external consequences: the baby gurgles and his mother laughs; he jumps up and down on her knee and she continues the bouncing; or he "sings" and his mother imitates and elaborates his song. In each gamelike interaction a link is forged between the baby's behavior and his mother's response, and it is the total of these links, together with others derived from contingency experiences with the inanimate environment, that form the basis of effectance motivation: "The world is responsive and I can make it respond."

The variety and frequency of the learning experiences are, understandably, important, but so is the promptness with which reinforcement follows response. Stuart Millar found that with six- and nine-month-olds a delay of only three seconds can completely prevent or disrupt the learning.[20] Where the intervening period was of one or two seconds, the infants could still make the link; anything longer was beyond the baby's capacity. Delayed rewards will appear haphazard to the baby and unconnected with his own activity; they are as likely to produce helplessness as no rewards at all.

CONCLUSIONS

The doctrine that babies live by maturation alone is now dead; but the simple view that adequate development requires stimulation turns out, after all, not to be very meaningful. Stimulation itself is too broad a concept—it needs to be analyzed according to type, amount, variety, intensity, regularity, duration, and timing. It is true, of course (and universally accepted), that babies need continuous and progressive interaction with their environment; the issue is rather by what kinds of input from the environment we can foster development.

The answer to this question cannot be made simply in terms of the amount of stimulation; "the more the better" does not do justice to the facts. Take the notion that the slow intellectual development of underprivileged children is due to understimulation. The slightest acquaintance with the type of environment in which such children are reared shows how far from the truth that must be. Quite on the contrary, these children tend to be subjected to a far *greater* overall level of stimulation: they are rarely alone, they are surrounded by a greater number of people in more crowded conditions, they hear more TV—the total amount of sheer noise impinging on them is likely to be quite considerable. Yet in a comparison of such children with a middle-class sample Jerome Kagan and Steven Tulkin found that the middle-class mothers were far more frequently engaged in face-to-face talk specifically directed at the baby.[21] The mother's talk, as far as the baby is concerned, is thus not merely a general background noise but a form of stimulation particularly meant for him and so challenging him to respond. Whether it is a matter of time or skill or motivation, such a mother can *personalize* the stimulation, ensuring that it connects up to the infant's internal state, his ability to attend, and his willingness to reciprocate. No wonder it seems linguistic development is fostered under such conditions.

5 / Mothering as Interlocution

Two people engaged in a conversation are participating in an extraordinarily complex social skill. For a conversation to be harmonious the participants must be attuned to each other; they must share the same code (or rather codes) of signals and be prepared to send and receive these signals via several channels simultaneously. They must not only share the same language and understand one another's vocabulary, but must also share the same nonverbal language by which we signal to each other such messages as "That's interesting—go on" or "Don't butt in yet, I haven't finished." Not only this, but they must be able to integrate their contributions into the temporal flow of the conversation. They have to share a set of rules for regulating their interaction, and though these rules may not be consciously formulated they are absolutely essential if communication is to proceed.

Interaction between mother and infant may also be thought of in this way. This would mean that, instead of considering *amounts* of maternal stimulation or attention or nurturance or of infant dependence or clinging or looking at mother, we should concern ourselves instead with the *temporal synchronization* of the two individuals' responses. Social interaction is never a "point event"; it always takes place over time and requires an ability mutually to integrate responses into one consistent flow. We may therefore ask whether this integration is already evident in the baby's interaction with his mother, how it is manifested, and by what means it is brought about. Interlocution, after all, is not only spoken dialogue; it is also nonverbal communication, even at an age before language has developed.

INTERPERSONAL SYNCHRONY

In Chapter Two we noted that infant behavior is organized from birth onward. Even apparently simple responses like sucking and looking are based on complex time sequences that impose characteristic cycles on much of an infant's spontaneous behavior. What is more, many of the infant's functions already show a fine degree of coordination with one another; sucking, swallowing, and breathing, for example, are integrated to form one system. *Intra*personal synchrony can thus be seen from the beginning, in certain respects even in the unborn fetus.

After birth, however, an infant is no longer surrounded by the relatively consistent conditions of the womb. In his new environment different kinds of adjustment are called for, and the most important of these concern the characteristics and routines of those who look after him. Accordingly a profound shift in the mechanisms that regulate synchronization takes place: the regularities of fetal life are replaced by the rather less regular and certainly much more varied phenomena of social life, and it is to aspects of the social environment that the infant's functions now become linked. And so the establishment of *inter*personal synchrony constitutes the primary task of early development.

This synchrony is achievable because, on the one hand, the infant, by virtue of his innate endowment, is equipped to participate in social interactions, while, on the other hand, his caregivers offer him the kind of stimulation that will appropriately enmesh their responses with his. From birth the infant therefore forms, potentially at least, a dyadic unit with his mother. How far potential is translated into reality will depend largely on the kind of opportunites with which the mother provides her infant for social interaction. But before analyzing more closely the dyadic activities of the mother, let us first examine the infant's contribution to mutuality.

Social preadaptation. If babies had no inborn preadaptation for interacting with others, social development could not take place as quickly as it does. At birth an infant is essentially an asocial being, in the sense that he still has no concept of people and responds only to crude features that may be inherent in other members of the species but are not exclusive to them. Yet just a few months later he not only has a concept of people, but he has begun the task of mastering the many social skills he will need as a member of his particular cultural group. That some sort of preparedness should pave the way is hardly surprising; after all, children are preadapted to deal with other aspects of the environment into which they are born—they have a breathing apparatus to deal with the air surrounding them from birth and a digestive system immediately able to cope with the food provided for them. So surely it is not absurd that they are also adapted to deal with that other vital aspect of their environment, people.

How does social preadaptation manifest itself? Two aspects can be distinguished, the structural and the functional. The baby has certain bodily structures that serve to bind him to other members of the species: a mouth, for example, precisely adapted to cope with the nipple that the mother provides; a visual apparatus that is highly sensitive to just those forms of stimulation (movement, pattern, contour, and so on) that emanate from other people—structures, in brief, that ensure a basic inherent compatibility between the infant and his parents.

But a mouth is more than a hole into which a nipple fits; once contact has been made, the infant must respond by sucking actively. Functional compatibility thus follows on from structural compatibility, and brings us back to the fact that an infant's behavior tends to be organized in particular ways over time. Many of his responses, as we have seen, conform to an on-off rhythm, and it is this that makes it possible for others to mesh their behavior with his. For one thing, there are indications that basic rhythms are shared by all human beings and may therefore be regarded as universal characteristics of the species. And, for another, an on-off pattern makes alternation between people possible, in that the pauses in an infant's behavior give the mother the opportunity to intervene and start up a rudimentary dialogue.

We shall look into the characteristics of these early dialogues later. First let us examine the basic rhythms that appear to underlie the behavior of us all. In analyzing the movements adults make while speaking, William Condon found that they could be reduced to units lasting just a fraction of a second.[1] Within each of these units the various parts of the body—head, eyes, fingers,

mouth, and so on—all moved in synchrony, sustaining a particular speed and direction for the brief duration of that unit before
all simultaneously changing to form another unit. These units,
according to Condon, underlie all behavior, for when he included
speech itself in his analysis he found the same units there, linked
to the rest of the movement pattern to form a total rhythm system. In addition, however, he found, in the first place, that a
similar rhythmic pattern could be discerned in the person *listen-
ing* to the speaker and, second, that this interpersonal synchrony
was evident even when that listener was a newborn baby. Infants, Condon maintains, move synchronously with adult
speech as early as the first day of life. From the beginning, their
behavior is linked to the behavior of adults.

A primal bond, based on a shared heritage containing both
structural and functional features, thus clearly exists between the
infant and his parents. Mutual interaction occurs smoothly not
because the infant is a lump of clay on which the mother can impose her own pattern at will, but because mother and infant
share the same pattern.

Social enmeshing. Whatever periodicities of behavior an infant is endowed with at birth, they do not continue unchanged
but soon become linked to the regularities of the external environment of which he is now a part. Just as plants that open and
close according to the amount of light available will adopt a regular day-night pattern, so the infant's rhythms will come to function in response to the patterning of the environmental events he
encounters. Indeed, as we have already seen, the waking-sleep-
ing alternation becomes "acculturated" very soon after birth and
thus represents one of the earliest examples of a circadian (that
is, a twenty-four-hour) rhythm.

The process whereby inherent rhythms come to be regulated
by external features is known as entrainment. An example is
provided by an early study by Dorothy Marquis, in which two
groups of infants were fed during the first ten days of life according to a three-hour or a four-hour schedule.[2] Within a few days
after birth a peak of restlessness had already developed just before the accustomed feeding time, and this became particularly
obvious when the three-hour group was shifted to a four-hour
schedule and so had to wait an extra hour for their feed. Thus we

can see how an inborn hunger rhythm becomes entrained by a feeding schedule determined by others. This constitutes a form of adaptation to social demands that must represent one of the earliest forms of learning.

The enmeshing of the infant's behavior with his mother's becomes particularly clear when we study their interaction at a highly detailed, microscopic level. Take an observation by Daniel Stern: three-month-old infants and their mothers, looking at one another face to face, move their heads strikingly in time with one another.[3] Film analysis reveals a pattern of mutual approach and withdrawal, according to which the infant turns his head away from his mother for a split second, mainly when she approaches him, and turns toward her as she withdraws from his visual field. Stern compares this pattern to a waltz, where certain steps and turns will be cued by one partner who leads, though in between both partners know the pattern well enough to move together.

Microanalytic studies of young babies and their mothers face to face can reveal a number of such mutualities. As we saw in Chapter Three, there is an innate regularity in an infant's looking behavior. In the social situation this regularity may still be present—indeed J. Jaffe and his colleagues have proposed that the time patterns of infant-adult gaze are the same as those found in adult verbal exchanges and so reveal some universal characteristic of human communication.[4] We are rarely conscious of these patterns, for they are so rapid that they can only be revealed by special techniques such as slowed-down films. Their importance as the basis of all direct social interaction, however, cannot be underestimated.

Just how the regularity in looking manifests itself depends not only on inherent processes in the infant but also on the kind of stimulation the mother provides. As Stern says, the three-month-old infant does not stare continuously at his mother's face but alternates between gazing at and gazing away from her.[5] This alternation shows some intrinsically determined patterning, but the precise duration of gazes-at and gazes-away depends primarily on the interest aroused by the mother, particularly on whether or not she is looking at the baby. If she is, the likelihood of his looking at her in turn is increased, thereby maximizing the occurrence of mutual gaze.

Numerous investigations of adults' social behavior have pointed out the intricacy of the mutual coordinations that occur in any face-to-face interaction. These coordinations, it appears, are not learned *de novo* by the young child; some at least are already discernible in the early weeks of life and are based on intrinsic regularities and rhythms shared with others.

Experience of dialogue. Most social interactions are based on alternation of roles—an on-off pattern where the two partners take turns in assuming the actor and the spectator role. One can detect this already in the infant's interaction with his mother, thanks first to the alternating nature of much of the infant's behavior and second to the mother's willingness to fit in with his sequential pattern.

Perhaps the earliest example of this sort of dialogue is feeding. Clearly, feeding a baby is not a onesided task like shoveling coal into a boiler. On the contrary, the infant is an active partner in determining just how the interaction should take place. Take Kenneth Kaye's observations: mothers interact with their infants in precise synchrony with the burst-pause pattern of sucking.[6] During bursts they are generally quiet and inactive; during pauses, on the other hand, they jiggle, stroke, and talk to the baby, and in this way take turns with him in being principal actor. Thus a mother allows herself to be paced by her baby: she fits in with his natural sucking pattern, responds to his signals such as ceasing to suck, accepts the opportunity to intervene offered by his pauses, and by this means sets up a dialogue between them.

The same pattern characterizes another kind of dialogue studied by Kaye, in which mothers attempted to teach their six-month-old infants a new skill (reaching round a barrier to obtain a toy).[7] The infants' visual attention in these circumstances was not continuous but followed a regular on-off pattern. Periodically the infant would look away from the task, whereupon his mother would promptly intervene and attempt to bring his interest back to it by demonstrating, moving his arm, or some other such strategy. The infant's gaze aversion thus acted as a signal to the mother and a turn-taking pattern was established.

These examples illustrate some of the features of early interpersonal synchrony. Responses are dovetailed so finely—they involve rhythms with beats of sometimes less than a second—

that they rarely reach conscious awareness. A mother can read the signals in her infant's behavior and as a result slot her own into the temporal pattern he creates. Most early interactions assume this form: T. Berry Brazelton and some colleagues found that, in mother-infant play, cycles of arousal could be discerned in the baby's behavior which occurred every few seconds and to which the mothers generally responded most sensitively with the appropriate approach or withdrawal, before then waiting for the baby to make the next move.[8]

From the very beginning, then, the infant's interaction with his mother assumes the form of a dialogue. In a sense, it is initially a onesided dialogue, for it depends very much on the willingness of one partner to let herself be paced by the other and follow his lead. It is nevertheless already a dialogue of exquisite precision in its patterning. This is clear in, for example, the vocal interchanges between mothers and infants, for these all have the air of a conversation—owing, above all, to the fact that the two individuals take turns. In a recent comparison of one-year-old with two-year-old children, we found the turn-taking pattern just as well established in preverbal infants as in those children who could sustain "real" conversations.[9] At both ages it was rare for both participants to vocalize simultaneously, and when they did it could well be quite intentionally, as in laughter or in chorusing (when one partner deliberately copies the sound the other makes). Otherwise all exchanges of speaker-listener role were managed with great precision, with a pause often of only a fraction of a second between the two utterances. This pattern is, of course, characteristic of adult conversations, in which each partner responds to the signals to exchange turns sent by the other and where simultaneous talking is avoided since it is difficult both to talk and to listen at the same time. It is therefore interesting to find "proto-conversations" even at a preverbal age. Again, however, it seems that it is the mother who is primarily responsible for the turn-taking pattern: it is she who waits for the infant to fall silent and then fills in the pauses, thus sustaining the interaction.

The growth of sociability. I have stressed that an infant's social behavior is preadapted, but let it not be thought that "everything is there" at birth, and let us not underestimate the interactional development that must follow. I have described this more fully elsewhere.[10] Here we need discuss only some of the land-marks that can illustrate the changes in the infant's behavior to which the mother must adapt herself in the course of the first year or two.

Above all, the child must acquire the *concept of a dialogue.* There are two aspects to this development: reciprocity and intentionality. As to reciprocity, we have seen that early dialogues tend to be onesided, in that the mother is primarily responsible for sustaining the interaction. Only later will the infant learn that the relationship is reciprocal, that the dialogue should be managed by both partners, and that the roles the two play are interchangeable (as for example in the give-and-take games that develop toward the end of the first year, which Jerome Bruner describes[11]). And intentionality develops because, through being involved in dialogues with other people, the infant learns that his behavior communicates—that his cries, his smiles, his vocalizations, indeed a great range of his behavior, will be attended to by others and produce particular effects on them. In time, therefore, he will send out such signals intentionally, in the definite expectation that they will be responded to. The infant in the early weeks of life may cry because he has a pain; eventually, however, he will cry to summon his mother to deal with the pain. Having learned to anticipate future effects he can now demand, summon, request, and plead.

But before he can do so effectively, two further developments are necessary. In the first place, there must be an increase in the sheer number of means of communication he can use. Certain primitive signaling systems are available from the early weeks, smiling and crying being the most obvious. Subsequently he develops other channels for interlocution: he learns the meaning of social gestures like pointing; he becomes capable of understanding the significance of the direction of gaze; and (most important of all) language evolves—not automatically with increased maturity but, as Bruner has argued, on the basis of the ability he already has to participate in sequences of interaction. Linguistic competence is preceded by communicative competence: the dialogue begins long before the first word is heard. With language, however, the flexibility of communication increases vastly.

And the final development that takes place concerns the cognitive processes on which the ability to interact with others is based. These include the ability to differentiate self from others, without which a true dialogue would be impossible; also object permanence—the ability to appreciate that other people and things have an existence of their own independently of whether one sees them or not; and finally an expansion of attention span, which enables an infant, say, to play ball with his mother rather than, as earlier, play with either his mother or a ball.

THE MOTHER'S INTERACTIVE TECHNIQUES

All these developments in the baby's social behavior occur because, again and again in the course of every day, the mother creates opportunities for her child to participate in many and various interactions. The baby cannot, for instance, learn about turn taking or develop reciprocal skills unless he is repeatedly involved in dialogue; indeed he can only learn that communication with others is possible if others are willing to communicate with him. From the very beginning he may be ready for social encounters, but it is up to his mother to structure these in order to maximize growth. How does she do it? We shall describe her contribution to the dialogue in terms of six types of maternal techniques.

Phasing techniques. John and Elizabeth Newson have described the way in which a parent tackles the task of getting a four-week-old to follow a dangling ring with his eyes. They explain that the parent must attend carefully, not just to the infant's general state of arousal but to his precise focus and line of regard:

> Having 'hooked' the attention of the infant upon the ring, one then begins gingerly to move it across his field of vision in such a way that the infant's eyes continue to hold the object with successive fixations until eventually the head follows the eyes . . . If the test object is moved too suddenly, or is left static too long, the visual attention of the infant will flag and the attempt will have to begin all over again from scratch. [12]

The adult must monitor his performance most skillfully and keep adjusting the position of the dangling ring, moment by moment, according to the infant's spontaneous actions.

This behavior is, in a sense, an example of what a mother is almost constantly doing with her child. Far from deciding independently upon her course of action and then arbitrarily imposing it upon the child, she continuously monitors his activities so that she can time her own interventions in synchrony with his. The infant, that is, is already engaged in some course of action and the mother, ever watchful, must decide when she must slot her responses into the stream of his behavior if she is to have any impact upon him. Thus a large proportion of early interactions tend to begin with the infant's spontaneous behavior and are continued by the mother's willingness, at the right time and place, to reply by elaborating, modifying, or repeating what he is doing. Above all, she must allow herself to be phased by his activity.

Let us take as an example the way in which mother and child come to pay mutual attention to some particular part of their environment. Put the couple into a situation that contains various new, attention-worthy things for the baby to look at (say on a bus or train or in a doctor's waiting room), and one will almost certainly observe the following pattern. The baby, sitting on his mother's knee, becomes absorbed in the more prominent features of his surroundings, craning his neck to stare at them, turning his attention from one to another and back again. The mother in the meantime keeps an eye on what he is doing and then, almost automatically, glances in the same direction to find the object of his interest. When he turns his head to look elsewhere she may very well turn hers too; all along she is monitoring the child's focus of attention and thus, by following where he leads, converting it into a focus of mutual attention.

Glyn Collis and I have demonstrated this phenomenon under experimental conditions, and our video-recording reveals clearly the mother's exquisite sense of timing—particularly considering the rapidity with which shifts of gaze can occur. [13] Mothers rarely follow every one of the infant's looks, but they normally remain sufficiently attuned to be continuously aware of the direction of his interest and are thus in a position to predict what he will do next (such as reach for the object). What is more, establishing mutual attention is often only the first step in a whole series: mothers may not only look where the infant is looking, but also may then comment on what he sees, label it, and in other ways verbally elaborate upon it. Thus mother and infant come to share experiences—a sharing generally instigated by the infant's spontaneous interest in his surroundings but established by the mother's allowing herself to be paced by the baby.

We have already seen the importance of this phasing in a mother's contact with her baby—as, for instance, in the way she times her stimulation to coincide with the pauses between her newborn's sucks. The same principle holds for older babies too. Mary Ainsworth and Sylvia Bell have stressed that the mother's sensitivity to the baby's rhythms, signals, pacing, and preferences is central to successful feeds: they point in particular to the importance of letting the infant himself decide the rate at which he is fed.[14] But perhaps the most vivid example is provided by Martin Richards, who made film sequences of mothers and babies smiling at each other and then analyzed them frame by frame.[15] Two points emerged. First, an infant's behavior in these circumstances goes through a definite sequence: he is, for example, quietly attentive while the mother smiles, then gradually becomes more and more active until, reaching a crescendo, he pauses a moment while looking at her—and then finally returns the smile. And the second point Richards noted was that the mother, during the infant's crescendo, generally stops all her activity, as though she were giving her baby time to come out with his smile. If she did not do so, if instead she continued to bombard the infant with unphased stimulation, then he would come tense and fretful and eventually begin to cry instead of smile.

Thus in many situations interaction is a matter of the infant leading and the mother following. Timing is all-important: if the mother wishes to produce a predictable outcome she must know when to intervene, not only how.

Adaptive techniques. As to the *how* of mothers' interactions, one need only watch a mother at play with her baby to notice that she does not behave at all as she would toward an adult. Her movements tend to be slower, her gestures more emphatic, her facial expressions more exaggerated, and her speech more intermittent and simpler in structure, with plenty of repetition. Even adults who are not parents will quite automatically change their behavior according to the age of the child they are with. Adaptive techniques of this sort ensure that an infant, who has only limited apparatus for processing new information, can assimilate the stimulation offered him.

Take one typical characteristic of a mother's behavior—its repetitiveness, both in what the mother says (her baby talk) and what she does with her head, face, and body. In an analysis of adults' behavior with three-month-old babies, Daniel Stern found that the stimulation they provided was highly ordered and could be described in terms of three types of units.[16]

The *phrase:* a single utterance or burst of movement, generally lasting less than one second. Vocalization and bodily movement can occur simultaneously, according to Stern, and thus form temporal units that are organized in fairly consistent burst-pause patterns.

The *run:* a series of phrases similar in content or duration. Stern found that most phrases were organized in such repetitions, so that much of the stimulation the infant receives from the adult's voice and movement is in fact part of a repeating sequence—the mother, for instance, saying "what a funny boy" over and over again, perhaps accompanied by the identical forward bobbing movement of the head.

The *episode of maintained interaction:* a series of runs, generally lasting a minute or two, during which the adult keeps to a definite tempo and holds his attention on the child. Each of these episodes is bounded by intervals, when the adult reappraises (rarely consciously, of course) the tempo appropriate to the infant's state and activities, and then pitches the next episode accordingly.

There are two implications to such an analysis. In the first place, it illustrates the highly ordered world that the mother provides for her baby. Insofar as each stimulus episode has its own tempo, the infant is experiencing stimulation that is structured and predictable rather than chaotic. He can therefore form expectations about what comes next within each episode, though the constant reappraisal that takes place between episodes ensures that the interaction does not get stuck but can shift gear at appropriate moments. And the second implication is the extent (highlighted once again) to which an adult quite naturally adapts his manner of interaction to the age of his partner. For one thing, so much repetition in phrase structure would not be found in the behavior between adults, and, for another, the phrases a mother provides her infant are only about half as long as those in adult-to-adult discourse whereas the pauses are almost twice as long. In other words, the mother acts as if the baby can take in smaller chunks of information at any one time than an adult, and needs more time to process each before receiving the next.

Facilitative techniques. It is already quite apparent that mothers are not at all the ever didactic creatures they used to be thought. On the contrary, they frequently allow their children to initiate interactions and set their pace, while they themselves are content to follow and to offer the stimulation they consider most appropriate to their baby's activities and perceived aims.

But mothers are not merely passive hangers-on, either. They too have aims and goals even in the most casual play situation, if only to ensure that the child can make the best possible use of whatever materials the task in hand requires. Watch a mother with her one-year-old sitting on her knee in front of a collection of toys: a large part of her time is devoted to such quietly facilitative and scene-setting activities as holding a toy that seems to require three hands to manipulate, retrieving things that have been pushed out of range, clearing away those things that are not at present being used in order to provide the child with a sharper focus for this main activity, putting things next to each other that she knows the child will enjoy combining (such as nesting beakers), turning toys so that they become more easily grasped, demonstrating their less obvious properties, and all along molding her body in such a way as to provide maximal physicial support and access to the play material. Even in the more structured care situations, such as feeding and bathing, the skillful mother achieves her goal not by imposing, ordering, and forcing but by so structuring routine and environment that grasping the spoon or putting it in the mouth are quite naturally incorporated into the sequence of activity.

This point was well made by Burton White and Jean Watts in their work on the development of competence in young children. From their home-based observations they concluded that the amount of time mothers spent in directly teaching their children was surprisingly small. Instead of plain instruction they tended to employ various "low-keyed facilitative techniques" that aimed generally to encourage the child's activity—suggesting things for him to do, helping him when in difficulty, supplying needed materials, participating in his activity, admiring his achievements, and so on. Indeed the most effective mothers were those who excelled at performing the functions of "designer and consultant"—those who could design a physical world, usually in the home, that was beautifully suited to nurturing the burgeoning curiosity of a young toddler: "These mothers very rarely spend five, ten or twenty minutes teaching their one- or two-year-olds, but they get an enormous amount (in terms of frequency) of teaching in 'on the fly', and usually at the child's instigation. Although they do volunteer comments opportunistically, they react mostly to overtures by the child."[17]

It is no coincidence that these descriptions are reminiscent of "discovery learning" in school and of the part teachers can play in creating a setting for fostering children's spontaneous explorations and inquiries. And it is also no coincidence that these facilitative measures appear to lead to surer developmental progress —for example, Katherine Nelson observes that a nondirecting parent who accepts a child's behavior—both verbal and nonverbal—facilitates the child's progress in language acquisition.[18] But in those cases where the parent takes a highly active role and directs his child, his behavior has an "interference effect" that delays the acquisition of new verbal skills.

Elaborative techniques. If the mother just passively followed her child's initiatives, however, it is doubtful whether he would ever proceed through the developmental stages. Rather, she follows in order to lead: she lets her child in the first place indicate his interest at the moment and then proceeds, within the child's own context, to elaborate on that interest. In this way she lets him select his own topic and then begins to comment, demonstrate, and explain.

Take the phenomenon of shared visual attention. We have already seen that a mother tends to monitor her baby's direction of gaze and then follows it, establishing a mutual topic of interest. Yet often this is merely the first step in a whole sequence of interactions: having ascertained the infant's focus of interest the mother may then elaborate upon it—fetching it if it is a toy out of reach, verbally labeling it, pointing out its features, demonstrating its functions. To take the second of these: from the very beginning a mother bathes her baby in language; to handle even the tiniest baby without talking to him seems unnatural. Thus for a whole year or more before the child himself becomes capable of uttering his first word he is constantly exposed to speech. But what the mother says is far from arbitrary: it is closely geared to the infant's own activity. He sees a dog, she observes his interest and looks too, and then comments: "Isn't that a nice doggy?" She thus adds a verbal dimension to his visual experience and, by introducing the label within the context of the child's own activity, provides him with the chance of associating sight and sound and so acquiring an appropriate vocabulary.

Initiating techniques. However frequently the child initiates the exchange (in White's and Watts's observations this occurred in about two thirds of instances), there are always occasions when a mother for some reason must take the initiative. Yet even then her behavior is generally tied closely to the child's and not arbitrarily imposed upon him.

If, for example, a mother wants to draw her child's attention to some feature of the environment, the obvious way to do so is to point. To understand pointing as a social gesture has, however, a characteristic developmental history, for during most of the first year of life infants tend merely to look at the outstretched hand. As Catherine Murphy and David Messer have found, mothers of, say, six-month-old babies will therefore rarely point to draw attention to the object, preferring to bring the object to the child or the child to the object. Or they may use special cues, for instance snapping their fingers in front of the infant's eyes and then leading his gaze gradually from the hand to the object. Even with older children, however, the mother will carefully time her pointing to ensure that she catches the child's attention or, should he be absorbed in something else, first call him or nudge him so that he becomes aware of her behavior. Having pointed she will then look back at the child in order to make quite sure that he is indeed following her.

Thus the mother continuously monitors the child's behavior. Even before initiating an exchange she will frequently first glance at the child to ensure that her behavior will be appropriate, and the particular tactics she chooses will be determined by her reading of his condition. Even when she takes the initiative her behavior can be understood only in the context of the constant two-way flow that must characterize any relationship.

Control techniques. There are some situations, of course, where it is necessary for the mother to be rather more assertive. This arises, for example, when she wants the child to do something that he might not otherwise do or, alternatively, to stop doing something she considers undesirable. Curiously, of the various maternal techniques I have listed it is these control techniques that have received most attention in the past—indeed they have frequently been thought to make up the whole process of socialization, as though the mother's task were simply one of direction. Control was also seen as an arbitrary imposition on the child, rather like hurling a thunderbolt. Now that we have developed an orientation toward the two-way flow of a relationship, however, together with a realization that much is revealed about the nature of this flow by studying it at a very detailed level, it is time to return to an old problem with new methods.

Consider the following example described by Gordon Wells.[19] A mother says to her two-year-old: "Put the lid on top of the basket." Her precise manner of making this statement is carefully geared to the child's capacity to understand. She heavily emphasises the word *lid*, simultaneously looking at it and pointing to it; she then pauses to check that the child has understood; and then she moves on to the second part of the utterance, emphasizing the word *basket* and again looking and pointing to the relevant object. Her directive is far from being a parade-ground command: it is delivered at a pace appropriate to the child's capacity, accompanied by nonverbal gestures providing extra help, and in any case probably delivered only when the mother feels sure the child's attention is on her. All along her behavior is precisely adapted to the requirements of her own particular child.

To what extent this synchronization is typical of all situations and all mothers remains to be established. When a child is about to pull a pan of boiling water down on himself his mother is hardly likely to provide a nicely slowed-down statement—but then sheer volume should ensure his attention! Even under normal conditions, however, there are likely to be mothers who simply are not sufficiently attuned to their children to communicate with them meaningfully, and in those cases the consequences for the children are bound to be unfavorable.

CONCLUSIONS

The six types of maternal techniques I have mentioned can roughly be arranged along a continuum from passivity to activity in the order in which they have been listed. Yet even at the active end of the continuum we have seen that the mother can hardly be described as a dictator who arbitrarily imposes and directs. Her relationship with the child is rather that of a partner, though a senior partner by virtue of being more experienced, more powerful, and more likely to have consciously formulated ideas about the purpose and direction of the interaction. She rarely does anything without being aware of her child's precise requirements or without adapting her behavior in that light. The younger the child, the greater her need to adapt in this way, and it is one of the wonders of nature that mothers (or almost any adult confronted by a small baby) can make these changes so naturally and spontaneously that they may not even be fully aware of what they are doing. This results in the fine degree of interpersonal synchrony that is so particularly evident when we study interactions microscopically. Whether we observe a baby feeding, playing, being bathed, changed, and put to bed, or merely being bounced on his mother's knee, we find a highly intricate pattern of interaction—a pattern that is based on the intrinsic organization of social behavior but that subsequently develops through the sheer experience of mutual contact.

This takes us a long way from the traditional view of socialization, which saw this process as a quite straightforward matter of indoctrination: of telling small children about the use of spoons and potties, about the importance of saying thank you and not killing the new baby. The child had to fit into his social group, so one had to shape his behavior accordingly. We can now see that one cannot change a child unless one begins within the context of his own behavior. Change cannot be imposed from outside; it can only start from within the relationship between parents and child and thus becomes a matter of mutual adjustment. The two modify each other continually; they grow with each other. Socialization is a two-way and not a one-way business: like education, it is essentially a joint venture.

6 / Love, Hate, and Indifference

We have examined four conceptions of mothering which summarize the empirical work carried out so far. There is, however, no suggestion that they cover all aspects of mothering. So what in particular is missing?

Ask any mother what she considers to be the essence of mothering and she will have no hesitation in replying: love. And yet, curiously, mother love has not yet become researchable. It is of course frequently mentioned, particularly in the popular child-care literature. It is widely regarded as essential to the child's development: John Bowlby, for example, considered it as necessary to mental health as vitamins and proteins are to physical health.[1] But the preoccupation with intellectual functioning which currently characterizes psychological research is also reflected in the study of mothering and particularly in the neglect of its more emotional aspects. We may pay lip service to the importance of love, but as yet we have not translated our respect into serious research.

THE INGREDIENTS OF LOVE

What is mother love? How does love show itself? It may seem a heartache, a lump in the throat, but can we ever get beyond singing about it or putting it into poetry? Love means emotional involvement with another person. It brings with it the capacity to experience a great range of feelings centered on its object, from infinite tenderness to fierce possessiveness, from a willingness to sacrifice oneself for the sake of the other's well-being to great surges of hostility and aggression. Being so involved means that what the other person is and does assumes enormous importance; the mother identifies with her child, considers him a part of herself, and so experiences both his joy and his suffering as her own. She delights in his achievements, for they become hers; she feels shame and annoyance when in some respect she thinks he fails. There is thus a close emotional intertwining of the two.

It is important to realize that a love relationship involves a heightening of *all* emotions, of negative as well as positive feelings. Hate is never far from love; the most affectionate mother can be capable of intense anger at her child. When Jack and Barbara Tizard compared mothers with nurses from residential institutions, they found that mothers not only provided more affectionate physical contact but were also more frequently really cross with their children and upset by their behavior.[2] An analysis of the nurses' talk showed that they rarely expressed either pleasure and affection on the one hand or anger and displeasure on the other; mothers can be expected to express both frequently. During intelligence testing, mothers often had to be asked not to prompt, assist, or berate their children; this was never necessary with the nurses.

Love means a preoccupation with its object: a wish to be in the other's presence, a great enjoyment of his company, a wish to possess him that is sometimes coupled with jealousy of others who share his attention, a dislike of being separated for long, and a continuing orientation even in his absence. In mother love we therefore have the reciprocal of the child's attachment, which is also rooted in a need for physical proximity. But the mother's actions are not merely a reaction to the child's need; they represent rather a genuine expression of her own requirements—witness the mother creeping up to her sleeping baby to steal a look, or the array of photographs of a grown-up son or daughter who has left home. We have given much attention in recent years to the child's side of the relationship, particularly by observing his behavior during enforced breaks in that relationship; yet this information has only rarely been complemented by including data from the mother's point of view about her need for "togetherness." Why is it that some mothers seem unable to let go of their children while others completely desert them? How possessive are mothers? Under what circumstances and to what extent are they willing to share the care and supervision of their children?

How do mothers respond when separated from their children? To these questions we have as yet no conclusive answers.

Love also means a heightened sensitivity to its object. Anyone who has ever been in love knows of the increased awareness it brings of the other person, of the absorption in him that makes it so much easier to sense his moods, feelings, needs, and wishes. To be attuned to the child is part of mother love—so much so, according to the popular though quite unverified example, that the child's whimper will wake his mother when a thunderstorm fails to do so.

Maternal sensitivity. Let us examine the mother's sensitivity to her child further, for it enables us to continue the discussion of interpersonal synchrony that concerned us in the last chapter.

Consider a mother suffering from postnatal depression. She sits apathetically with her baby on her knee, staring vacantly around her and hardly noticing his behavior. He wriggles uncomfortably, but she takes no action to mold her body to his; he whimpers but she fails to investigate the cause of his distress. There is no feeling in anything she does, she is drained of emotion and quite incapable of any involvement with her offspring. The constant flow of his behavior means nothing to her: his responses have no signal value, for she is too encapsulated in her own feelings to be aware of the child's.

Love brings with it sensitivity. Without it one cannot sustain the intent awareness of the other that makes possible the very prompt response to and anticipation of his behavior that we have found to exist between mother and baby. As Mary Ainsworth has pointed out, underlying a mother's sensitivity is the ability to see things from the infant's point of view; it involves an empathy that is dependent on the mother's developing beyond egocentricity, and this, it appears, is an achievement that not every mother has successfully accomplished.[3]

In an attempt to account for some of the variation in infant behavior, Ainsworth developed a sensitivity-insensitivity scale, which is worth quoting in full:

> This scale deals with the mother's response to the infant's signals and communications. The sensitive mother is able to see things from her baby's point of view. She is tuned-in to receive her baby's signals: she interprets them correctly, and she re-

sponds to them promptly and appropriately. Although she nearly always gives the baby what he seems to want, when she does not she is tactful in acknowledging his communication and in offering an acceptable alternative. She makes her responses temporally contingent upon the baby's signals and communications. The sensitive mother, by definition, cannot be rejecting, interfering, or ignoring.

The insensitive mother, on the other hand, gears her interventions and initiations of interactions almost exclusively in terms of her own wishes, moods, and activities. She tends either to distort the implications of her baby's communications, interpreting them in the light of her own wishes or defences, or not to respond to them at all. [4]

According to Ainsworth, it is possible to rate mothers on a sensitivity-insensitivity continuum and then to demonstrate relationships between this rating and various aspects of infant behavior. Thus sensitive mothers are found to have secure babies who are able to explore strange situations, using the mother as a safe haven to whom they can return from time to time; and they are also able to tolerate brief everyday separations from her from time to time. The babies of insensitive mothers, on the other hand, either show such heightened insecurity that they cannot let the mother out of their sight or else, on the contrary, are unable to use the mother as a secure base in their play and exploration which, instead, they tend to pursue as though she were not present.

Sensitivity-insensitivity may not be a unitary trait, and giving a mother a score that represents her standing along this dimension could well obscure important variations in her behavior according to time and place. But as a primarily descriptive device that may help us to establish functional relationships between mothers' behavior and infants' response, maternal sensitivity has in fact emerged as a characteristic that appears to be centrally important. And insofar as sensitivity appears to be a precondition for successful infant development, mothers ought to be sensitive and insensitivity can be regarded as pathological. From this point of view, the fairly substantial minority of insensitive mothers in Ainsworth's admittedly small sample is of some concern. Some, she suggests, are too often oblivious to the infant's signals because they are fatigued, depressed, or compulsively preoccupied with other activities; others perceive the signals but misinterpret them, perhaps distorting them according to their own needs. Some mothers resent the infringement on their own autonomy, while others actively try to control their babies instead of letting them take the initiative. But love must be other-centered: where a mother habitually—all mothers do it occasionally—can go in and out of a room, preoccupied with other thoughts, and not even acknowledge her baby's existence, or when she arbitrarily pushes herself on him in response to her own needs instead of his signals, the process whereby his behavior becomes intertwined with his social environment will surely be seriously handicapped. Love, after all, is more than a warm and cosy feeling: it is expressed tangibly and affects the child in terms of his mother's pleasure in his company, her interest in him as a separate being, and her awareness of his communications and willingness to respond to them. Without these the child's rearing will take place in an atmosphere of indifference.

IS LOVE INEVITABLE?

Mother love has often been called an instinct—regarded, in other words, as something bound to be there irrespective of circumstances, an inevitable consequence of having a child. But do the facts bear this out?

Some loveless people. Let us first turn to the Ik, a small tribe living on the northern border of Uganda and most sensitively described by Colin Turnbull, an anthropologist who lived among them for a period.[5] The Ik had formerly been a nomadic tribe of hunters and gatherers but, as a result of government action, had been excluded from their most fertile hunting grounds and confined to a limited, barren area in which they were no longer able to support their existence adequately. With starvation came a virtual disintegration of their social organization: the family as an institution almost ceased to exist, and in the wake of the struggle to remain alive there followed an utterly selfish attitude to life that displaced all positive emotions like love, affection, and tenderness.
The selfishness and indifference considered acceptable among the Ik may astonish those used to other ways of life, in particular

since it was mainly directed toward those we usually regard as in greatest need of care and solicitude—the very young and the old. There was, according to Turnbull, simply no room in the lives of these people for such luxuries as family sentiment and love. Children were regarded as useless appendages who were turned out of the parents' hut when they reached the age of three years, compelled from then on to make their own way without help or guidance from any adult and certainly without any parental love or affection. Consequently one rarely saw a parent with a child except accidentally or incidentally; when a child hurt himself by falling into the fire, the only reaction was amusement; if a predator came and carried off a baby, the mother was merely glad at no longer having to care for it. One never saw a parent feed a child over the age of three—on the contrary, such children were regarded as competitors from whom food had to be hidden; if consequently one died of starvation, that merely meant one mouth less. Mistrust, cruelty, and selfishness thus became the primary interpersonal emotions; there was no place for love— not even between parent and child.

Are the Ik unique? Can we dismiss them merely as a curious aberration without parallel? Unfortunately not. Take Margaret Mead's description of the Mundugumor people of New Guinea: here too there is no such thing as mother love, for from birth on a baby finds himself in a society with an intense dislike of children—finds himself there, that is, if he is allowed to survive, for many babies are simply thrown into the river.[6] Dislike is expressed in all the attitudes and rearing practices the child encounters: in the quick and peremptory way in which he is suckled, in the sullen resentment with which the mother greets any sickness or accident that may befall him, and in her refusal to let him cling to her in fear or affection.

The origin of these patterns of lovelessness is a matter for conjecture. According to Turnbull, the crucial factor for the Ik is the need to survive in the face of starvation. According to Mead, on the other hand, it is the abundance in which the Mundugumor live that is primarily responsible, in that it requires practically no cooperation among individuals and thus leaves plenty of scope for violent hostilities to flourish in their social life—to which the affectionless upbringing of children is, of course, so precisely adapted. Let us not pursue these conjectures; what matters to us is the fact that two societies can apparently function completely without any of the basic affectionate emotions that we assume to be inherent in humanity. Lovelessness has become institutionalized; parents dislike and resent their children, and the inevitability of mother love has therefore to be questioned.

But can we not escape this conclusion by pointing to the peculiar circumstances of these two primitive societies and insisting that they are of no relevance to us? Are not parents in civilized societies different? Surely such people do not neglect, ill treat, or kill their children. Unfortunately one look at official statistics will show how prevalent such phenomena are even in Western society. The number of children annually taken into public care in Britain, for example, because of parental cruelty or neglect or desertion, is too great for these cases to be written off as exceptional aberrations. And for that matter, what of those (variously estimated as between 300 and 600 in Britain) who are actually killed every year by their parents?

The battered-baby syndrome has sprung to prominence only in recent years, for previously it was too difficult to accept the idea that a substantial number of parents in our midst are capable of injuring, maiming, or even murdering their children. Some facts about such cases are now beginning to emerge. In particular, it is widely agreed that violence usually results from the combination of three forces in the parents' lives: emotional immaturity, which makes it difficult for them to deal with stress; various financial, social, and occupational problems, which they find insoluble; and finally some characteristic of the battered child that singles him out as a likely victim.

The third factor is particularly relevant to us, for it illustrates again the interactive nature of what goes on between parent and child. It is not simply that some aggressive adults will pick on any child who happens to be around. There is evidence, for example, of an association between prematurity and battering, the suggestion being that premature babies are less likely to initiate a maternal response that might prevent battering. Similarly, the battered baby is frequently a sickly child who is difficult to rear and so makes extra demands for care that his parents are not able to meet. One of the commonest reasons a parent will give for a battering incident is that the child had been crying excessively, that nothing could stop him, and that as a result the parent finally lost his temper and went berserk. How near hate and aggression lie to love must have been experienced by any parent who has ever had to deal with a two-year-old in the midst of a raging temper tantrum that nothing can apparently bring to a stop; only some inner control prevents most parents from becoming batterers. When, however, a parent does not have the emotional maturity to cope with a stressful challenge from a child, assault and injury may follow. The child's conditions acts on the parent's inadequacy.

CONDITIONS AFFECTING MOTHERING

If love is not inevitable, if a whole society can be without any of the signs of affection, tenderness, and self-sacrifice that we consider the hallmarks of the parent's relationship to the child, we must ask what the conditions are under which love does manifest itself. Let me say straight away that as yet we know extraordinarily little about these; I shall therefore single out just some of the possibilities that seem likely candidates.

Personality factors. Some individuals, for reasons of personality, may have considerable difficulty in functioning as parents. The most extreme examples are people with mental illness: schizophrenia, for example, can cripple the capacity to deal with others and will probably introduce all kinds of distortions into the relationship with a child. Depression too can be crippling, though it is much less likely to assume severe and permanent forms. This applies also to anxiety states: sometimes it is possible to contain the condition sufficiently so that the mother, however ill she may be, can still function adequately as a mother. It is obviously dangerous to assume that, just because an individual has psychiatric problems, they will affect all aspects of living, including the parental role.

Paradoxically, many personality factors not falling into the recognized pathological range may have far greater implications for the relationship with the child. I have repeatedly stressed the central role of sensitivity; I now also stress that the insensitive parent is perhaps the greatest obstacle to the child's developmental progress, for he is likely to be more attuned to his own wishes and desires than to those of his child. Being egocentric, he will have a distorted view of the child's capacities and may well attempt, in a rigid and authoritarian manner, to force the child into a mold that he just will not fit. Some of the overprotective mothers described by David Levy, whose treatment of their children had such various profound effects, clearly fall into this category: having certain fears and anxieties of their own, they projected them on to their children and then proceeded to treat them accordingly.[7]

Environmental conditions. Enough experience has now accumulated among professional workers for us to conclude with confidence that certain environmental conditions are likely to have a detrimental effect on mothering. Poverty, poor housing, unemployment, malnutrition, poor health: these are some of the factors that give rise to stress and anxiety and may impair a mother's treatment of her children. But care must be taken with statements about cause and effect: bad conditions are often associated with inadequate parental personalities, and it may well be these that actually do the damage. Nevertheless, it is certainly true that mothering skills can best be exercised only in a decent environment, and it may be that without one even the best of parents may fail.

Hormonal influences. If certain animals like sheep and goats are separated from their newborn offspring immediately after birth for even a few hours, serious distortions in maternal behavior result. On reunion the mother may butt her infant away and refuse to care for it, or she may treat it no differently from any other strange young animal. It has therefore been suggested that the hormonal changes following parturition bring about a critical period immediately after birth during which the mother must be with her offspring. If she is not, mothering atrophies.

We have already seen the danger of applying such simple, cut-and-dried notions to human development. Nevertheless, these findings have raised queries about the way maternity hospitals customarily keep mothers and babies apart during the first few days of life, except for feeding times. In a series of reports Marshall Klaus and his colleagues compared a group of mothers permitted only the routine contact with their babies with another group given extended contact—their naked babies were allowed in their beds for an extra five hours on each of their three days in hospital.[8] Interviewed and observed one month and again one year later, the two groups revealed a number of differences. The mothers of the extended-contact group were found to be more reluctant to leave their babies with others, to be more responsive to their crying, to engage in more eye-to-eye contact during feeds—to be generally rather more preoccupied with their babies. That just fifteen hours' additional contact in the first three days should produce such effects detectable one year later seems remarkable; it should be added, however, that these were just a few of very many effects measured, and that the groups were similar in far more ways than they were different. There are also difficulties with the way that kind of study is run, particularly when interviewers and observers know which group each mother belongs to and may accordingly be biased in their assessments. Although Klaus went some of the way to deal with methodological loopholes, he does not appear to have taken all the essential precautions, so it is too early to accept and implement these findings. And there are other contradictory findings that make caution doubly advisable.

In a study of premature babies, A. D. Leifer and some colleagues examined what is perhaps the most extreme form of early separation, which arises when a baby has to stay in an incubator for an extended period.[9] Mothers of such babies were randomly allocated to two groups: in one, the standard hospital procedure was employed, according to which each mother was permitted only to look at her baby during his several weeks in the incubator; in the other group, mothers were permitted to handle their infants in the incubator from the second day on. Observations of the mothers one week and one month after discharge from the hospital, made during normal care-taking routines, failed to reveal any consistent differences between the two groups. So the notion that a mother's attachment may be seriously affected by a temporary separation immediately after her baby's birth remains without firm support.

And this is just as well, for what hope would there otherwise be for adoptive parents and their children? If mothering were completely dependent in some simple way on hormonal changes that occur only in conjunction with childbirth, adoption would need to be discontinued since it would be producing a lot of affectionless and empty relationships. For that matter, one can hardly maintain that giving birth is *bound* to give rise to maternal love: the Ik and the Mundugumor tell us otherwise, and so will many a mother in our own society who found that falling in love with the baby did not happen immediately but took weeks. Human development—of mother as well as of child—is more complicated and allows more room for variation than such mechanical models would indicate.

Childhood deprivation. A rather more likely explanation for the development of mothering is that is stems from the mother's own childhood. Love, in other words, develops early on in life on a reciprocal basis, in that the experience of being loved by one's parents elicits the capacity for love in the child, enabling him to return the feeling and later also to transfer it to others. Being loved makes him fit for love; not having this experience will stunt his ability.

Harry Harlow's description of the behavior of "unmothered mothers" has, in the case of rhesus monkeys, vividly illustrated the stunting effect of childhood deprivation.[10] Animals brought up in isolation were found in adulthood to be grossly deficient in all forms of social behavior, and particularly in their mothering: either they were completely indifferent to their offspring, not feeding, grooming, and retrieving but ignoring them, or they became baby batterers, displaying violence that was alarming to watch. Even with animals, it appears, mothering is not inevitable —even here it will not emerge except under certain developmental conditions.

Is maternal competence in humans also the end result of a particular developmental history? Are distortions of mothering brought about by deficiencies in the mother's own upbringing? We do not know the answers for sure, though much social-work experience suggests that deprived mothers are more liable to have deprived children. There are, however, too many other possible causes in these problem families for us to be sure that the right answer is entirely psychological. But we can be certain that mothering is not an instinct in the sense of an inherently determined behavioral pattern that will manifest itself blindly and automatically irrespective of circumstances. It is, rather, a set of abilities and feelings which, though based on the mother's inherent propensity to interact with others, will manifest itself only under particular social conditions. Discovering what these conditions are remains an urgent task for research.

Knowledge and ignorance. It is often argued that deficiencies of mothering are, in some part at least, due to ignorance. For instance, a report by the Department of Health and Social Security in Britain suggests that "many parents do not understand how to play, talk, read and generally communicate with their children and to interpret the various stages of development— mental, emotional, physical and social—through which all children go."[11] Thus the isolation of the nuclear family has been held responsible for robbing mothers of the opportunity of learning from their own mothers and from other experienced women in the community. Similarly the disappearance of the family with large numbers of children is said to have deprived older girls of the apprenticeship they formerly served in caring for their younger siblings.

To some extent this may be true. But is mothering really just a skill that can be taught or acquired by observing others? Is it a matter of formal knowledge that can be conveyed by more or less formal means? Let me stress first of all that there is certainly a great deal of factual information that can usefully be made available to parents. How to convey such information responsibly, without the distortion or oversimplification that professional popularizers are so prone to, is a major problem; but how actually to change behavior that most needs changing is quite a different problem.

The trouble is that one can't teach love in night school. One can convey factual information by this means, or by books and magazines and TV programs, though probably only the more intelligent, educated, and interested sections of the community will read or tune in. More important, those aspects of the mothering process most likely to give rise to developmental problems are not amenable to this treatment. A sensitive mother will quickly realize that an inappropriate technique needs changing, for by definition her sensitivity involves a constant watch on the effects of her behavior and a willingness to change in the light of these effects. But what if there is no sensitivity?

As we have seen, a great deal of the mother's interactive skill takes place at a micro-level and is normally performed automatically and without planning, in response to signals that she does not verbalize and of which she may not even be consciously aware. We simply do not know whether a mother deficient in this skill for one reason or another can be taught how to phase her behavior to that of her baby. Any form of explicit instruction, oral or written, is almost certainly going to be unsuccessful. Teaching would need to be informal and individualized and ought to take place in relation to particular children and their particular problems. Even then such instruction, however tactfully carried out, might defeat its own end by deadening spontaneity, making adaptability mechanical, and reducing interaction to a set of formal rules. At present we do not know enough to answer such doubts; attempts to launch relevant schemes on an experimental basis would be well worth while.

THE HIGH-RISK COUPLE

Up to now we have been discussing the mother at risk: the deprived, the mentally ill, the rigidly authoritarian woman. But we should recognize that difficulties in mothering may just as likely originate from the child's characteristics: there are, it is true, rejecting mothers (in the sense that women would have difficulties with any child), but there are also rejecting babies—those, for instance, who will remain tense whatever one does with them, who cannot be comforted by anyone, or who will fret and cry whenever they are picked up and held. It is easy to blame the mother, to attribute fault to her as though everything the baby does is her responsibility (a notion based, of course, on the clay-molding view of socialization). Yet one must recognize that there are some children who by nature are more difficult to rear than most, some who from the beginning are emotionally so much more vulnerable that they make far greater demands on a mother's ability. And for that matter there are some (found principally among the brain-injured, the autistic, and the mentally handicapped) who may be almost impossible to mother in the usual sense, for their capacity to enter a reciprocal relationship may be so impaired that normal mutuality cannot develop.

But, continuing to regard mother and baby as a pair, it is by and large more useful to think of *couples* at risk than of *individuals* at risk. We acknowledge in this way that there are mother-child pairs who fail one another—whatever the origin of their problem. It is in fact often difficult to disentangle causes by the time a couple with a distorted relationship presents itself for therapeutic action. In any case, if therapeutic action is to be effective one needs to recognize that the difficulty mostly lies *between* the partners rather than *within* either one or the other. As we have seen in the case of baby battering, it is the combination of parental immaturity with some pathological characteristic of the child that underlies the assult; similarly it is such combinations as sickly infant and overanxious mother, ambitious parent and retarded child, fearful and sensitive son and emotionally tough and unfeeling father, which are most likely to give rise to difficulties. There is little point in apportioning blame in these cases; even to suggest that it should always be up to the parent to adjust to the peculiarities of the child may be asking for the impossible. Parents, like children, are not lumps of clay—they too are not infinitely adaptable and with the best will in the world may not be able to transcend certain limits of endowment and upbringing. I have said much about respecting the child's individuality, and now make the same plea for mothers and fathers. If, for example, a mother cannot abide the idea of breast-feeding she should not be forced to do it, for whatever benefits the child may obtain will be more than outweighed by the consequences of distorting the mother's preferred behavior. Fortunately both mothers and babies can adapt to one another within quite wide limits; nevertheless, limits do exist, and the normally natural and spontaneous match between their two sets of responses can fail to take place. The ill-matched couple thus becomes the high-risk couple.

CONCLUSIONS

Mother love is not inevitable. It is not a necessary part of human nature like breathing, for whole societies can function without it, in a way that may be abhorrent to us but which does show that love is not an integral part of humanity itself. Even with animals it is necessary to create the conditions necessary for the growth of love. We cannot assume that the qualities associated with mother love will simply emerge; if we wish to foster these qualities in humans, we must actively create the conditions that make their growth possible.

Much urgent work needs to be done to discover precisely what these conditions are. Only when that is done can we create the right circumstances for fostering maternal competence. Educational programs, counseling, and therapy are short-term and superficial measures compared to this much more fundamental task. Not that they should be neglected—it is just that their part is marginal in comparison with finding and improving the basic foundations on which love is built. And if these do turn out to be mainly concerned with developmental antecedents along the lines indicated by Harlow's monkeys, and if, in human beings too, adequate mothering can be shown largely to result from being adequately mothered, the task is indeed a long-term one that will outlast several generations.

Let us note, however, one respect in which active progress is now being made in the improvement of mothering. This is in the choice of being a parent in the first place. Choice of parenthood depends, first, on the availability of birth-control techniques and, second, on social expectations about married people having children. Thanks to technological advances in contraceptive methods, it is now possible to choose when or whether to have children, even though a great deal still needs to be done in spreading the use of contraception to those countries most in need of limiting their populations. Less progress has been made in changing the social norm that all married couples ought to have children. For a long time it has been expected of every husband and wife that they would, as a matter of course, produce children, and it used to be regarded as a cause for shame if they failed to do so, whatever the reason. In times of high infant mortality it was, of course, important to ensure a sufficient supply of children to maintain the population. At the present time, when our main concern is with overpopulation, the social pressures brought to bear on parents to produce children are no longer similarly relevant. Married couples ought not to consider it a *duty* to bring children into the world; procreation ought not to be a matter of convention whereby every family consists of two parents and two or three children. With increasing occupational and social outlets for women, a wife need no longer disappear into the confines of the home on marriage, with nothing to do except have and care for children. Couples can now free themselves both of the physical inevitability of producing children and of the social pressures that force parenthood on them as a duty. Having children should be only for those who want children and will actively enjoy children. There can be no better way of improving the quality of motherhood than to make it genuinely a matter of choice.

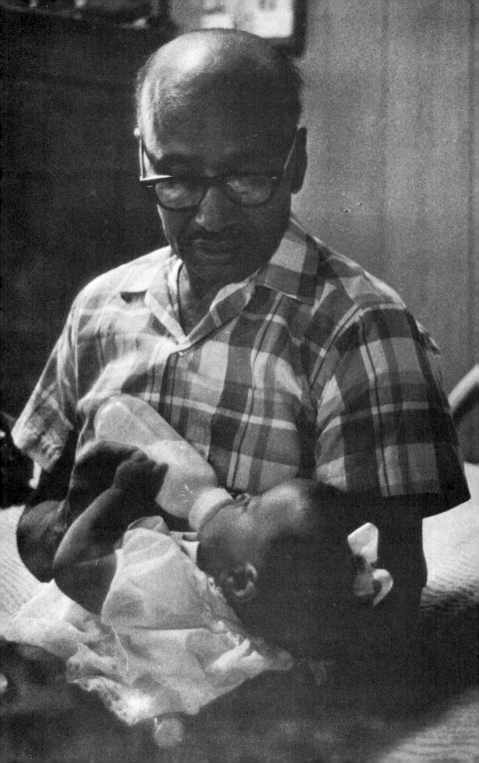

7 / Do Babies Need Mothers?

There are two ways of finding out about mothering. One is to look at mothers; the other is to look at children without mothers.

MATERNAL DEPRIVATION

Research on maternal deprivation raises two principal issues: the long-term consequences on personality development and the immediate effects on the child's behavior.

Long-term consequences. John Bowlby's contention that a warm, intimate, and continuous relationship with the mother is essential in the early years if pathology is not to develop is as controversial and unsettled today as it ever was.[1] The capacity to care and feel deeply about others may be potentially available to every child but, according to Bowlby, unless it is elicited and sustained without any break in the first two and a half years of life, it will atrophy and the child's ability to form personal relationships will be severely affected. Unbroken mother love, in other words, is vital during this period; any amount of subsequent love cannot make up for earlier deficiencies.

So far, few systematic studies have unequivocally supported this contention. Examining children institutionally reared for the first few years of their lives and then adopted, Barbara Tizard was unable to find any evidence of gross pathology in their social behavior.[2] They showed some tendency to be overfriendly with strangers, but the great majority had no difficulty in forming normal ties of affection with their adoptive parents—even well after the supposed critical period for forming relationships.

For that matter, Bowlby himself failed to find confirmation of long-term effects: in a sample of preadolescent children who had been hospitalized by tuberculosis for lengthy periods in the first two years of their lives, he found no obvious sign that the capacity for relationships was in any way inferior to that of similar nonseparated children.[3]

Once again we see that early childhood experiences, even when they span the so-called crucial first few years, do not necessarily produce irreversible effects. But what if the deprivation is not limited to the early years, what if it continues so that the child never has the opportunity to form a bond with a mother-figure? Both Harlow's work with monkeys and the miscellaneous clinical experience of social workers and psychiatrists suggest that such circumstances may well cripple for life an individual's capacity to love. Bowlby's "affectionless character," in other words, is an individual who cannot give love to others because he has never known love throughout childhood, early or late. But we cannot make even this connection with complete confidence: for one thing, there are few systematic studies on which to base any conclusions, and for another one finds so many other possibile contributory causes in such cases that it is often difficult to know what part each played. All we can assert at the moment is that it seems a lot more plausible that fifteen years of deprivation should result in a deprived personality than that two and a half years should.

Immediate consequences. When we turn to the immediate effects of a child's separation from his mother, the picture is much clearer. A young child is likely to experience severance of the bond with his mother as devastating—if, that is, the separation occurs under tra umatic conditions and the child is sent to a strange environment and is there looked after by strangers, as happens, for instance, in hospitalization or admission to public care. Detailed observation has revealed three sequential phases for most children in these circumstances: first a period of distress, when the child cries for his mother and refuses to be looked after by anyone else; then a period of despair, during which he becomes quiet and apathetic; and finally a period of detachment, when he appears to come to terms with the situation but at the cost of his emotional tie with his mother and his ability to put his trust into any relationship. There can be a number of variations on this theme—if, for example, a substitute mother is available he may become attached to her in the third phase. Nevertheless, children between approximately six months and five years of age are most likely to react in this way to separation. In addition, when the separation is temporary, the child is further unsettled for a period when he returns home: he may initially continue to be detached and treat his parents like strangers, though subsequently he will go to the opposite extreme and become overdependent and clinging, refusing ever to be left alone.

Whatever the psychological mechanisms behind these reactions, they show how traumatic separation can be. In the light of this alone—despite the more controversial issue of the long-term consequences—any practical steps that can be taken to minimize the grief and distress involved are fully justified. Thus children's hospitals have modified their attitudes toward parents' staying with their children, allowing extended visiting or even rooming-in; children's residential institutions have also become more personalized, for instance by adopting family groupings; and, most important of all, public-welfare authorities have adopted a policy of prevention, so that every effort is made to keep the children at home and avert the need to admit them to hospital or residential care.

Research on the effects of separation provides a vivid indication of the strong emotional forces that bind the child to his mother. It is a pity, however, that no comparable studies have illustrated the effects on the mother. The almost exclusive attention on the child may suggest, if not that the mother is unaffected by the experience, at least that she is left unchanged by it. Yet Robert Hinde has shown that in rhesus monkeys the post-separation disturbance found in infants is caused primarily by the distortions separation brings about in the *mother's* behavior. These animals' capacity for precisely synchronized interaction breaks down during the separation period, so that for a while after reunion the mothers are unable to continue the relationship quite as before. It is highly unlikely that similar clear-cut effects can be found in human mothers. Nevertheless the animal data underline the fact that it is the *couple* that has become separated and not just the child, and that both individuals rather than just one must subsequently readjust.

THE EXCLUSIVENESS OF MOTHERING

Are we to conclude from studies of separation that one of the mother's main functions is to provide ever-present physical security, and that this function cannot be filled by anyone else? Is the child's attachment exclusively and absorbingly to her alone? Does she fail the child by not being with him throughout each and every day? The answer depends largely on the nature of the child's attachment.

Attachment development. Social development in infancy may be thought of in terms of three basic steps:

> The infant's initial attraction to other human beings that makes him prefer them to inanimate features of the environment.
> His learning to distinguish among different human beings so that he can recognize his mother as familiar and strangers as unfamiliar.
> His ability, finally, to form a lasting, emotionally meaningful bond with certain specific individuals whose company he actively seeks and whose attention he craves, though he rejects the company and attention of other, strange individuals.

If the infant is to attain mature social behavior he must accomplish each of these three developmental steps. He will make them in the sequence given: first, differentiation of human beings as a class apart from the rest of the environment; second, recognition of certain individuals as familiar; and third, formation of specific bonds. The last must, of course, await the first two: the baby must recognize his mother before he can become attached to her. These two accomplishments are, in fact, separated by a considerable gap of time, for there are indications that an infant can learn to distinguish his mother from other people within the first three months, and yet not till many months later are there signs that a lasting, specific bond has been formed with her. In the intervening period the infant may "know" his mother and still be content with the attention offered by others. Attachment is thus the end product of a long-continuing process.

The third step usually takes place at around seven months. At that age we first see signs of what must be regarded as one of the major developments in early life, the ability to miss the absent mother. Before this age we find no upset at a separation, whether it is a major one such as hospitalization or a minor, everyday one such as being left alone in a room at home. It is true that an infant in his first half-year, left by the mother to his own devices, may after a while begin to fret, but it is likely to be attention and stimulation in general that he needs and any person may satisfy him. Subsequently, however, people cease to be interchangeable: attention has to be supplied by specific familiar individuals, for strangers may be met at least initially with wariness or outright fear. And the baby no longer simply responds to the mother when she is physically present, but actively seeks her when she is not.

Are we to conclude that separations before this age are of no consequence? In view of the grief and distress experienced from that time on it is apparent that, where there is a choice of timing, any separation ought to occur before the vulnerable age is reached. This is possible with certain types of hospitalization (for instance, those for elective surgery). Adoption and other procedures involving a change of mother-figure should also be carried out where possible within the first half-year.

There is one reservation, however, that we ought to bear in mind. In the past, separation studies have exclusively concentrated on relatively gross indications such as crying, changes in activity, and sleeping or eating disorders. But in view of the fine synchronization established between mother and baby from the early weeks on, we should consider the possibility that at a much more microscopic level interactive processes can also be disrupted before seven months. Even if the infant reveals no awareness of the mother's absence and therefore shows no separation upset, might not established synchronization patterns be distorted when someone else takes the mother's place—someone who has not learned the specific characteristics of that particular infant, who may not have the motivation to be as sensitive to his signals as his mother, and whose own behavior in interaction may be entirely different? If this were the case, some sort of effect would register in the infant's behavior, though the indications might well be far more subtle than those in separated infants beyond the seven months' milestone. It may be, of course, that an infant can initially discriminate only the behavior that *any* human might produce—rather as a very small baby will smile at any pair of eyes regardless of whose they are. In that case anyone with a certain minimal skill in handling babies should be able to take the mother's role at that early period of life.

All this is, of course, purely speculative; what is required now are studies that examine at a much more microscopic level the effects of changing the mother-figure.

Multiple attachments. With whom does the infant form an attachment once he becomes capable of it? Until recently the conventional view of the mother-infant bond stressed above all its exclusiveness. It was thought essential for a child's mental health that his care should be monopolized by a single mother-figure. And in any case, the child was thought unable initially to form specific attachments to more than one person—and that person was, of course, his ever-present mother.

Empirical investigations have revealed the truth to be rather different. An infant is not confined to just one bond, as Bowlby suggested: once he has reached the stage of forming specific attachments, he is capable of maintaining a number at the same time. Peggy Emerson and I, investigating this question, found that 29 percent of our sample of infants, when they first became capable of forming specific attachments, formed several simultaneously, and that 10 percent formed as many as five or more.[4] By eighteen months 87 percent had formed multiple attachments, and almost a third of them five or more. Grandparents, older siblings, neighbors, but above all fathers were singled out. Moreover, being attached to several people does not necessarily imply a shallower feeling toward each one, for an infant's capacity for attachment is not like a cake that has to be shared out. Love, even in babies, has no limits.

There is, we must conclude, nothing to indicate any biological need for an exclusive primary bond; nothing to suggest that mothering cannot be shared by several people. The nature of attachment may vary considerably from individual to individual, ranging from an exclusive concentration on one mother-figure to a distribution among many. Just what form it takes appears largely to depend on two influences: the social setting and the personalities of the individuals within that setting.

Attachments and the social setting. For the most striking example of the way in which social structure influences the behavior of the young, let us turn to two species of monkeys, the pigtail and the bonnet, which have been vividly described and contrasted by Leonard Rosenblum.[5] Bonnets are essentially gregarious creatures who spend long periods of the day huddled together in compact groups, each animal in passive contact with several others. When a mother gives birth she almost immediately reunites with the group, and other adults can touch and handle the newborn without protest. Among pigtails, on the other hand, adults are rarely in close physical contact with one another. The only groupings one does find are closely knit family units of mothers and children; otherwise there are few contacts between members of the troop. After giving birth, a pigtail mother not only remains separate from the group but also vigorously attacks any animal that approaches her infant. When the infant subsequently attempts to leave the mother to explore his surroundings she restrains him or, if he succeeds, promptly retrieves him. Unlike the bonnets with their much less differential pattern of caregiving, these animals foster a close and exclusive bond.

These differences in group living become absorbed into the overall differences in infant experience. They provide the social context within which the patterns of maternal and infant behavior peculiar to each species occur. Thus, even when older, the pigtails reveal a much more enduring and selective relationship with their mothers than the bonnets. When a bonnet infant is separated from his mother, his response to her loss is slight, for he quickly establishes contact with other adults who in turn are immediately willing to provide him with substitute care. A pigtail infant becomes extremely agitated, searches for the lost mother, and eventually develops severe and enduring depression. The birth of a sibling shows up similar differences: while the bonnet reacts only minimally, the pigtail becomes disturbed and even more clinging. Even the nature of play distinguishes the two species: since bonnets have many opportunities to interact with other young, their play is primarily social; pigtails, having few such opportunities, engage mainly in nonsocial, "exercise" play.

It is not difficult to translate these observations into human terms and find the equivalent situations where a child's care is, respectively, wholly in the hands of one mother-figure or distributed among several. Whereas among lower animals the social setting is largely specific to each species, in human society there is great variety in family life, for biology does not constrain us to the same degree and (in theory at least) we are free to choose among different types of social setting in which to rear our children. As we see from studies of kibbutz-reared children, like those of Bruno Bettelheim, a rather different personality structure results from group rearing than from traditional, family-oriented rearing.[6] So what type of personality development do we wish to foster—do we want bonnet children or pigtail children? Which is better?

There is obviously no scientific answer to such a question. It involves a value judgment that must be made by society, not by psychologists. All the latter can do is discover what types of outcome result from rearing within different social settings and put the facts before society. Unfortunately, in the past value judgments have commonly been dressed up as mental-health judgments: children had to be brought up as pigtails or else their capacity for social living was said to be stunted. That might be true—but only as long as society was committed to the pigtail type of social living. A bonnet-reared child is unlikely to become an effective pigtail parent; any particular cultural tradition rests on continuity between childrearing, personality development, and social setting. Yet that is very different from equating any one such tradition with mental health and all other traditions with ill health. The notion that a child's attachments cannot safely be distributed among several figures must be challenged: the course of such a child's personality development may well be different, but who dares say it will be "worse" in any absolute sense?

From the wider perspective of an anthropologist, Margaret Mead has been able to compare those societies where an exclusive maternal relationship is usual with those (such as the

Samoan) where mothering activities are diffused among a number of females of all ages.[7] There can be little dispute that where there is diffusion the child is "insured" for possible loss of mother; there will be greater continuity of care arrangements and less liability of trauma. The "bonnet pattern" is clearly useful to a society with a high death rate (and it may well be that the shallow level of feelings one finds in adult interpersonal relationships in Samoa is useful for the same reason). There is certainly little doubt that the great feeling of group belongingness which Bettelheim describes as developing among kibbutz children is very well suited to a society that requires a close-knit, armed membership willing to put the general cause before individual considerations. Again, care is required in making judgments about childrearing in relation to an absolute standard of mental health which may in fact merely reflect the norms of Victorian society.

Attachments and personality characteristics. Neither a mother's responsibility for a child's physical care nor her constant availability can guarantee that an attachment will actually be formed. Sometimes a child will become intensely attached to his father or an older sibling, though he cannot see them so often, and sometimes his mother, though a constant companion, comes rather low on his preference list. The person a child chooses to become attached to depends on the adult's behavior in interaction—on subtle qualities like sensitivity, responsiveness, emotional involvement, and probably others we know little about.

What we can say with confidence, though, is that it is these personality attributes (whatever they may turn out to be) that are the essential adult contribution to bonding—and not kinship. Mother need not be the biological mother: *it can be any person of either sex.* The ability to rear a child, to love and cherish and care for him, is basically a matter of personality: the so-called blood bond is a complete myth. There is nothing to suggest that firm attachments cannot grow between children and unrelated adults who take over the parental role—by fostering or adoption, for instance. The notion that the biological mother, by virtue of being the biological mother, is uniquely capable of caring for her child is without foundation.

There is, for that matter, no reason why the mothering role

should not be filled as competently by males as by females. The human male's relative lack of involvement in childrearing is essentially a cultural rather than a biological phenomenon. Originally, of course, biological factors were involved, in particular the fact that it is the mother who gives birth to the child and that it was she who subsequently had to suckle it for many months to come. Child care of necessity used to be women's business. Add to that the need to use the superior strength of the male to hunt, work the fields, and make war, and one finds sufficient reasons for the division of labor almost universal in former times and still prevalent today. Yet technological progress, in this respect as in so many others, can free mankind from biological constraints and make possible new patterns of social living. Technology has perfected milk formulas and the feeding bottle so that anyone, of either sex, can satisfy a baby's hunger. That same technology has provided us with so many mechanical aids that sheer physical strength is now rarely needed: women can just as well press the button that starts an agricultural harvester or fires a nuclear rocket. And, finally, biologists give us reason to think that even the process of birth, in its natural form, is not sacrosanct—that it may eventually be possible to grow a fetus not in a womb but in an artificial environment from which it is delivered in due course. Thus all the original reasons for confining child care to women are disappearing: mother need not be a woman.

The question is often asked: what is the role of the father in the family? The answer is simple: just what he and his wife choose it to be. If we accept that there are now no operative biological constraints that confine motherhood to one sex and make women of necessity more capable caregivers, then we must agree that nothing but tradition sends men out to work and keeps women at home. Role segregation is no longer as absolute as it was just a few decades ago: women do go out to work and men increasingly participate in domestic tasks, including childrearing. Occasionally necessity dictates the parents' action, as when an unemployed father takes charge of home and children while his wife goes out to work. But ideally personality characteristics should decide: some fathers, by virtue of temperament and disposition, may make better mothers than their wives, just as some women may be more capable breadwinners than their husbands. Thus, in an ideal child's world, convention would be replaced by personal inclination: whichever parent displayed those qualities that made him or her the best match for the child would be in the more favorable position to become primary caregiver. But so much the better, of course, if both parents are equally capable of this task. From the child's point of view, it matters little what sex mother is.

Consistency of care. Given that an infant can form multiple attachments, and that these depend more on the quality of interaction than on its sheer daily duration, there is no need to prolong the controversy about whether the mother must be the infant's constant companion throughout each and every twenty-four-hour day. Clearly some minimum period of togetherness is required, but there is nothing absolute about how much. Beyond the minimum, it is the personal qualities the adult brings to the interaction that matter most. Provided these can be given full play, there is no reason why mother and infant should not spend a portion of the day apart—the mother at work, the child at some form of day care, or in some other arrangement with which the family is comfortable. It may well be, of course, that such arrangements place a greater onus on the mother to get thoroughly acquainted with her baby during the limited time they spend together; it may also be, as Simon Yudkin and Anthea Holme have pointed out in their survey of working mothers, that the exhaustion of doing a full-time job will make it difficult for the mother to respond sensitively to the child in the short time they are in each other's company at the end of the day.[8] But these considerations need to be weighed against the disadvantages of the mother's not going out to work or the child's not being sent to day care. Certainly reviews like that by Yudkin and Holme have found no ill effects as far as the children of working mothers are concerned; indeed, some of these children are said to be more self-reliant and less anxious than the children of mothers who do not work. And certainly children can, without any adverse effects, accept care and attention from a subsidiary attachment figure for part of the day during the absence of the primary attachment figure.

There is, however, one important proviso, and that concerns the stability of arrangements made for a child's substitute care. When the people responsible for the child keep changing, he could well be disturbed as a result. A child may not require *uniformity* of care but he does need *consistency* of care. The world must be a predictable place for him, particularly where the people he sees daily are concerned. Never to know from one day to the next who will be "mother" makes for confusion. Consider the experience of the institutionalized children described by Jack and Barbara Tizard: an average of twenty-four persons had been responsible for their care during the first two years of life, compared with an average of just over two for a family-reared group observed in their study for contrast.[9] No wonder that caregiving in institutions tends not only to be multiple but also detached, for when a child has a casual encounter with a "mother" he may soon never see again, the emotion he invests in the interaction is likely to be minimal.

CONCLUSIONS

Do babies need mothers? Yes—if it means that they need to be involved in a love relationship, that satisfaction of their physical wants alone is not enough. No—if it means that mother must be the one who gave birth, that no other person can take her place. No again—if we take mothering to involve an exclusive care relationship that must encapsulate the child's total social and emotional life; on the contrary, there are many arguments for allowing a child to widen his interpersonal horizon from the beginning and for not discouraging other attachments. And finally yes—if we mean that a limited range of familiar people should provide consistent care throughout the years of childhood.

There can be little doubt that past research on the early stages of children's social development has involved too exclusive a focus on the bond with the mother, as though that represented the totality of their interpersonal life. Insufficient attention has been paid to the influence of others who also turn out to play important roles even in infancy. This situation is changing now: for instance, the work of Urie Bronfenbrenner on the influence of other children in later childhood, especially in certain cultural settings, has recently been acknowledged and related to the course of personality development.[10] Similarly the changing nature of family life is forcing us to take note of other figures who play a part even early on, particularly fathers whose involvement in child care is gradually becoming much greater than it used to be. And, once we are willing to take these other figures into account and realize that infants can form attachments to them too, it becomes very much easier to distinguish the factors that play little if any part in bond formation (the blood relationship, the provision of food, constant availability), and concentrate instead on the particular qualities in the adults' behavior that result in love relationships.

The exclusive focus on the mother and the failure to take into account other social influences in a young child's environment may well be another reason for the fact that the childrearing studies described in Chapter Two predicted later personality so poorly. These studies concentrated only on what mothers did and felt: the suggestion that an infant's relationship with, say, his five-year-old sister or the friendly woman living next door might contribute to his later personality would have been regarded with derision. Yet all we are learning of human psychological development suggests that end results are rarely due to single causes, however potent they may seem at the time. Mothers, without doubt, are in an excellent (and usually the best) position to influence their child's development, but the older sibling and the woman next door may well leave their mark too.

Society is changing rapidly in many ways, some of which have direct implications for childrearing. The nuclear family is neither as sacrosanct nor as rigidly set in its role structure as it was in Victorian times. Mothers go out to work, fathers bathe babies, people decide to live in communes or kibbutzim, and society's involvement in the childrearing process—by way of care provision and education—is constantly being extended. But children will always need mothering, whatever the social milieu in which they live, and to understand in precise detail the emotions, functions, and effects involved in this process remains one of our more urgent tasks if we are to improve the conditions under which early development takes place.

References

2 Childrearing and Early Experience

1. B.M. Caldwell, "The Effects of Infant Care." In M.L. and L.W. Hoffman, eds., *Review of Child Development Research, 1* (New York: Russell Sage Foundation, 1964).
2. H.R. Schaffer and P.E. Emerson, "The Development of Social Attachments in Infancy," *Monographs of Social Research in Child Development,* 1964a, *29,* no. 94.
3. R.R. Sears, E.E. Maccoby, and H. Levin, *Patterns of Child Rearing* (Evanston, Ill.: Row, Peterson, 1957).
4. E.S. Schaefer, "A Circumflex Model for Maternal Behavior," *Journal of Abnormal and Social Psychology,* 1959, *59,* 226-235.
5. M.R. Yarrow, J.D. Campbell, and R.V. Burton, *Child Rearing: An Inquiry into Research and Methods* (San Francisco: Jossey-Bass, 1968).
6. J.B. Watson, *Behaviorism.* (New York: People's Publishing Company, 1925).
7. R.A. Hinde, "The Nature of Imprinting." In B.M. Foss, ed., *Determinants of Infant Behaviour, 2* (London: Methuen, 1963).
8. E.H. Erikson, *Childhood and Society* (New York: Norton, 1950).
9. W. Dennis, *Children of the Creche* (New York: Appleton-Century-Crofts, 1973).
10. J. Kagan and R.E. Klein, "Cross-Cultural Perspectives on Early Development," *American Psychologist,* 1973, *28,* 947-961.
11. A.D.B. Clarke, "Learning and Human Development," *British Journal of Psychiatry,* 1968, *114,* 1061-1077.
12. B.A. Campbell and J. Jaynes, "Reinstatement," *Psychological Review,* 1966, *73,* 478-480.

3 The Organization of Infant Behavior

1. A.H. Parmelee, W.H. Wenner and H.R. Schulz, "Infant Sleep Patterns from Birth to 16 Weeks of Age," *Journal of Pediatrics,* 1964, *65,* 576-582.
2. E. Aserinsky and N. Kleitman, "A Motility Cycle in Sleeping Infants as Manifested by Ocular and Gross Bodily Activity," *Journal of Applied Physiology,* 1955, *8,* 11-18.
3. H.F.R. Prechtl and D.J. Beintema, "The Neurological Examination

of the Full-Term Newborn Infant," *Clinics in Developmental Medicine, 12* (London: Heinemann, 1964).

4. S.J. Hutt, H.G. Lenard and H.F.R. Prechtl, "Psychophysiological Studies in Newborn Infants." In L.P. Lipsitt and H.W. Reese, eds., *Advances in Child Development and Behaviour, 4* (New York: Academic Press, 1969).

5. P.H. Wolff, "The Role of Biological Rhythms in Early Psychological Development," *Bulletin of the Menninger Clinic,* 1967, *31,* 197-218.

6. P.H. Wolff, *The Causes, Controls and Organisation of Behaviour in the Neonate* (New York: International Universities Press, 1966).

4 Mothering as Stimulation

1. A.L. Gesell, *Infancy and Human Growth* (New York: Macmillan, 1928).

2. W. Dennis, *Children of the Creche* (New York: Appleton-Century-Crofts, 1973).

3. P.H. Wolff, *The Causes, Controls and Organisation of Behaviour in the Neonate* (New York: International Universities Press, 1966).

4. C. Lamper and C. Eisdorfer, "Prestimulus Activity Level and Responsivity in the Neonate," *Child Development,* 1971, *42,* 465-474.

5. Wolff, *The Causes, Controls and Organisation of Behaviour in the Neonate.*

6. A.F. Korner, "Neonatal Startles, Smiles, Erections and Reflex Sucks as Related to State, Sex and Individuality," *Child Development,* 1969, *40,* 1039-1053.

7. D.M. Levy, *Behavioral Analysis* (Springfield, Ill.: Thomas, 1958).

8. A.F. Korner and R. Grobstein, "Visual Alertness as Related to Soothing in Neonates: Implications for Maternal Stimulation and Early Deprivation," *Child Development,* 1966, *37,* 867-876.

9. A.F. Korner and E.B. Thoman, "Visual Alertness in Neonates as Evoked by Maternal Care," *Journal of Experimental Child Psychology,* 1970, *10,* 67-78.

10. Y. Brackbill, G. Adams, D.H. Cromwell and M.L. Gray, "Arousal Level in Neonates and Preschool Children under Continuous Auditory Stimulation," *Journal of Experimental Child Psychology,* 1966, *4,* 178-188.

11. Y. Brackbill, "Acoustic Variation and Arousal Level in Infants," *Psychophysiology,* 1970, *6,* 517-526.

12. Y. Brackbill, "Cumulative Effects of Continuous Stimulation on Arousal Level in Infants," *Child Development,* 1971, *42,* 17-26.

13. Wolff, *The Causes, Controls and Organisation of Behaviour in the Neonate.*

14. A. Thomas, S. Chess, H.G. Birch, M.E. Hertzig and S. Korn, *Behavioral Individuality in Early Childhood* (New York: New York University Press, 1964).
15. H.R. Schaffer and P.E. Emerson, "Patterns of Response to Physical Contact in Early Human Development," *Journal of Child Psychology and Psychiatry*, 1964b, 5, 1-13.
16. S.K. Escalona, *The Roots of Individuality* (Chicago: Aldine, 1968; London: Tavistock, 1969).
17. H.A. Moss, "Sex, Age and State as Determinants of Mother-Infant Interaction," *Merrill-Palmer Quarterly*, 1967, 13, 19-36.
18. M. Lewis, "State as an Infant-Environment Interaction: An Analysis of Mother-Infant Interactions as a Function of Sex," *Merrill-Palmer Quarterly*, 1972, 18, 95-122.
19. J.S. Watson, "Smiling, Cooing, and 'The Game'," *Merill-Palmer Quarterly*, 1972, 18, 323-339.
20. W.S. Millar, "A Study of Operant Conditioning under Delayed Reinforcement in Early Infancy," *Monographs of the Society for Research in Child Development*, 1972, 37, no. 147.
21. J. Kagan and S.R. Tulkin, "Social Class Differences in Child Rearing During the First Year." In H.R. Schaffer, ed., *The Origins of Human Social Relations* (London and New York: Academic Press, 1971).

5 Mothering as Interlocution

1. W. Condon, "Speech Makes Babies Move." In R. Lewin, ed., *Child Alive* (London: Temple Smith, 1975; New York: Doubleday, 1975).
2. D.P. Marquis, "Learning in the Neonate: The Modification of Behavior under Three Feeding Schedules," *Journal of Experimental Psychology*, 1941, 29, 263-282.
3. D.N. Stern, "A Micro-Analysis of Mother-Infant Interaction: Behavior Regulating Social Contact Between a Mother and her 3-1/2-month-old Twins," *Journal of the American Academy of Child Psychiatry*, 1971, 10, 501-517.
4. J. Jaffe, D.N. Stern and J.C. Peery, " 'Conversational' Complexity of Gaze Behaviour in Pre-Linguistic Human Development," *Journal of Psycholinguistic Research*, 1973, 2, 321-330.
5. D.N. Stern, "Mother and Infant at Play: The Dyadic Interaction Involving Facial, Vocal and Gaze Behaviors." In M. Lewis and L.A. Rosenblum, eds., *The Effects of the Infant on Its Caregiver* (New York: Wiley, 1974).
6. K. Kaye, "Toward the Origin of Dialogue." In H. R. Schaffer, ed., *Studies in Mother-Infant Interaction* (London and New York: Academic Press, 1977).
7. K. Kaye, "Maternal Participation in Infants' Acquisition of a Skill"

(unpublished dissertation, Harvard University, 1970).

8. T.B. Brazelton, B. Koslowski, and M. Main, "The Origins of Reciprocity: The Early Mother-Infant Interaction." In Lewis and Rosenblum, *The Effect of the Infant on Its Caregiver.*

9. H.R. Schaffer, G.M. Collis and G. Parsons, "Vocal Interchange and Visual Regard in Verbal and Pre-Verbal Children." In H.R. Schaffer, ed., *Studies in Mother-Infant Interaction* (London and New York: Academic Press, 1977).

10. H. R. Schaffer, *The Growth of Sociability.* Baltimore: Penguin, 1971; Schaffer, ed., *Studies in Mother-Infant Interaction.*

11. J.S. Bruner, "The Ontogenesis of Speech Activities," *Journal of Child Language,* 1975, *2,* 1-19.

12. J. and E. Newson, "On the Social Origins of Symbolic Functioning." In V.P. Varuna and P. Williams, eds., *Piaget, Psychology and Education* (London: Hodder and Stoughton, 1976).

13. G.M. Collis and H.R. Schaffer, "Synchronisation of Visual Attention in Mother-Infant Pairs," *Journal of Child Psychology and Psychiatry,* 1975, *16,* 315-320.

14. M.D.S. Ainsworth and S.M. Bell, "Some Contemporary Patterns of Mother-Infant Interaction in the Feeding Situation. In A. Ambrose, ed., *Stimulation in Early Infancy* (London and New York: Academic Press, 1969).

15. M.P.M. Richards, "Social Interaction in the First Weeks of Human Life," *Psychiatria, Neurologia, Neurochirurgia,* 1971, *74,* 35-42.

16. D.N. Stern, "The Infant's Stimulus World During Social Interaction," In Schaffer, *Studies in Mother-Infant Interaction.*

17. B.L. White and J.C. Watts, *Experience and Environment, 1* (New York: Prentice-Hall, 1973).

18. K. Nelson, "Structure and Strategy in Learning To Talk," *Monographs of the Society for Research in Child Development,* 1973, *38,* no. 149.

19. G. Wells, "The Contexts of Children's Early Language Experience," *Educational Review,* 1975, *27,* 114-125.

6 Love, Hate, and Indifference

1. J. Bowlby, *Maternal Care and Mental Helath* (Geneva: World Health Organization, 1951).

2. J. and B. Tizard, "The Social Development of Two-Year-Old Children in Residential Nurseries." In H.R. Schaffer, ed., *The Origins of Human Social Relations* (London and New York: Academic Press, 1971).

3. M.D.S. Ainsworth, "The Development of Infant-Mother Attach-

ment." In B.M. Caldwell and H.N. Ricciuti, eds., *Review of Child Development Research*, *3* (Chicago: University of Chicago Press, 1974).

4. M.D.S. Ainsworth, S.M. Bell and D.J. Stayton, "Individual Differences in Strange-Situation Behavior of One-Year-Olds." In Schaffer, *The Origins of Human Social Relations*.

5. C. Turnbull, *The Mountain People* (London: Jonathan Cape, 1973).

6. M. Mead, *Sex and Temperament in Three Primitive Societies* (New York: Morrow, 1935).

7. D.M. Levy, *Maternal Overprotection* (New York: Columbia University Press, 1943).

8. M.H. Klaus, R. Jerauld, N.C. Kreger, W. McAlpine, M. Steffa and J.H. Kennell, "Maternal Attachment: Importance of the First Post-Partum Days," *New England Journal of Medicine*, 1972, *286*, 460-463; J.H. Kennell, R. Jerauld, H. Wolfe, D. Chester, N.C. Kreger, W. McAlpine, M. Steffa and M.H. Klaus, "Maternal Behavior One Year after Early and Extended Post-Partum Contact," *Developmental Medicine and Child Neurology*, 1974, *16*, 172-179.

9. A.D. Leifer, P.H. Leiderman, C.R. Barnett and J.A. Williams, "Effects of Mother-Infant Separation on Maternal Attachment Behavior," *Child Development*, 1972, *43*, 1203-1218.

10. H.F. and M.K. Harlow, "The Affectional Systems." In A.M. Schrier, H.F. Harlow, and F. Stollwitz, eds., *Behavior of Non-Human Primates*, *2* (New York: Academic Press, 1965).

11. Department of Health and Social Security, *The Family in Society* (London: HMSO, 1974).

7 Do Babies Need Mothers?

1. J. Bowlby, *Maternal Care and Mental Health* (Geneva: World Health Organization, 1951).

2. B. Tizard and J. Rees, "The Effect of Early Institutional Rearing on the Behaviour Problems and Affectional Relationships of Four-Year-Old Children," *Journal of Child Psychology and Psychiatry*, 1975, *16*, 61-73.

3. J. Bowlby, M.D. Ainsworth, M. Boston, and D. Rosenbluth, "The Effects of Mother-Child Separation: A Follow-Up Study," *British Journal of Medical Psychology*, 1956, *29*, 211-247.

4. H.R. Schaffer and P.E. Emerson, "The Development of Social Attachments in Infancy," *Monographs of Social Research in Child Development*, 1964a, *29*, no. 94.

5. L.A. Rosenblum, "Infant Attachment in Monkeys." In H.R. Schaf-

fer, ed., *The Origins of Human Social Relations* (London and New York: Academic Press, 1971).

6. B. Bettelheim, *The Children of the Dream* (New York: Macmillan, 1969; London: Thames and Hudson, 1969).

7. M. Mead, "A Cultural Anthropologist's Approach to Maternal Deprivation." In *Deprivation of Maternal Care: A Reassessment of Its Effects* (Geneva: World Health Organization, 1962).

8. S. Yudkin and A. Holme, *Working Mothers and Their Children* (London: Michael Joseph, 1963).

9. J. and B. Tizard, "The Social Development of Two-Year-Old Children in Residential Nurseries." In Schaffer, *The Origins of Human Social Relations.*

10. U. Bronfenbrenner, *Two Worlds of Childhood: U.S. and U.S.S.R.* (New York: Russell Sage Foundation, 1970; London: Allen and Unwin, 1971).

Suggested Reading

Tony Booth, *Growing Up in Society* (London: Methuen Essential Psychology, 1975). A general discussion of the influences that determine the way in which people grow up together. It takes into account not only the contribution of psychology but of such other social sciences as sociology, anthropology, and social history. Its main value lies in the way child development is seen as occurring within the social context of each particular culture.

Kurt Danziger, *Socialization* (Baltimore: Penguin, 1971). Danziger provides an account of the different conceptions of socialization and discusses some of the topics that have been studied under this heading, such as moral development, sex-typing, and social-class influences.

Penelope Leach, *Babyhood* (Baltimore: Penguin, 1975). An account of early development which aims to relate research findings to the practical everyday problems faced by parents.

Roger Lewin, ed., *Child Alive* (New York: Doubleday, 1975; London: Temple-Smith, 1975). Various researchers summarize what we have learned about the nature of child development in recent years. The book as a whole emphasizes the psychological sophistication of even quite young babies.

Harry McGurk, *Growing and Changing* (London: Methuen Essential Psychology, 1975). Considers some of the fundamental issues in attempts to understand children, in particular the concept of development and the role of theory, the methods employed in studying developmental processes, and the relative contributions of heredity and environment.

Michael Rutter, *Maternal Deprivation Reassessed* (Baltimore and New York: Penguin, 1972). Rutter looks at one of the most controversial topics in child development and systematically reviews the evidence that has accumulated on the effects, both short- and long-term, of early deprivation of maternal care.

Rudolph [H. R.] Schaffer, *The Growth of Sociability* (Baltimore: Penguin, 1971). An account of work on the earliest stages of social development. It shows how sociability in the early years has been studied, and reviews what we have learned about the way in which a child's first social relationships are formed.

Index